SURVIVOR KID

SURVIVOR KID

A PRACTICAL GUIDE TO WILDERNESS SURVIVAL

DENISE LONG

Library of Congress Cataloging-in-Publication Data
Long, Denise.
  Survivor kid : a practical guide to wilderness survival / Denise Long.
    p. cm.
  Includes bibliographical references and index.
  ISBN 978-1-56976-708-5
  1. Wilderness survival—Juvenile literature. I. Title.

  GV200.5.L66 2011
  613.6'9—dc22

                            2011004952

Cover and interior design: Andrew Brozyna, AJB Design, Inc.

Cover images: Kelly V. Brozyna [front top]; Alaska Stock [front left];
    PunchStock [front right]; Steve Lowtwait [back right].

Illustrations: Andrew Brozyna [pp. 5, 10, 21–23, 26–35, 44, 47–49,
    60, 62, 74, 109, 114, 119, 120, 149 (top), 150 (bottom), 151, 152, 162,
    163, 170 (bottom), 171]; Steve Lowtwait [pp. 11, 19, 54, 56, 66, 95,
    161, 166, 167, 169, 170 (top), 179–187]

Published by Chicago Review Press, Incorporated
814 North Franklin Street
Chicago, Illinois 60610

ISBN 978-1-56976-708-5

Printed in the United States of America
5 4 3 2 1

TO the kids in my neighborhood who love the outdoors as much as I do, to my friends who insisted I write this book, and especially to all the nice people in search and rescue.

CONTENTS

INTRODUCTION

The shivering woke me up. My entire body shook and my teeth chattered uncontrollably. It was still dark, and my dog and I were alone in the woods, huddled together in a hastily built bark-and-branch shelter. And it was cold—really cold. I had no sleeping bag or blanket, and the temperature had dropped to 15 degrees Fahrenheit in the dark forest. I tried to get a sip of water, but my water bottle had frozen solid. "Let's get up," I told Moxie, my German shepherd. We wriggled out of the tiny shelter and I began to walk unsteadily in place while Moxie stretched and looked for a place to pee. My frozen boots felt like they were made out of rocks—but, as the blood began to flow through my limbs, I stopped shaking and my brain started to work again. For the umpteenth time that long night, I checked my watch, hoping for the miracle of approaching daylight. It was only 3:00 A.M. We still had hours to go before we'd see the sun. I stood in the frigid night air and listened to a great horned owl somewhere above me for a minute, then crawled back into my tiny shelter. I pulled Moxie to me and wrapped a tarp over us. With my face pressed against her dusty fur, I promised, "Just a few more hours, and we'll be warm."

Moxie and I were not lost; I had volunteered to spend the night alone with her in a remote forest as part of our search and rescue training. This was the second time I was being tested on my shelter-building skills. Each time, I was not allowed to have a fire or any sort of comfort item, and the temperature was well below freezing. No one could call these practice sessions comfortable, but I did learn that I could survive wintry nights if I was caught outside.

Now you can, too. In fact, the information in this book will help you to survive all kinds of situations you might face if you become lost in the wilderness someday. You won't need to know how to shoot a deer with a homemade arrow, clean and cook it, and turn its skin into a waterproof tarp. You just need to know how to stay healthy and out of trouble until rescuers find you. I've taught middle school students how to do just that—the same lessons taught to adults in survival classes. Just because you're young, you do not need to be babied. You can handle it.

This book is for young adventurers who want to build up their survival skills and learn what to do if they ever find themselves lost or in a dangerous situation in the wild. Does that sound like you? Great—let's get started!

1

ANYONE CAN GET LOST
(and What to Do If It Happens to You)

Anyone can get lost or have an emergency while hunting, hiking, or playing in the wilderness. It happens to kids and adults—even experienced hunters and hikers—and occurs most often during simple day hikes or quick outings. That means that this chapter is the most important one in the book. Maybe you skipped it at first so you could read about the fun stuff—building different kinds of shelters, identifying animal tracks, or creating a solar still. (I probably would have done the same thing!) All that other stuff is important, but none of it is as crucial as what you'll learn in this chapter. You need to read this section carefully, and you may want to talk to a parent about what you have learned.

The most important things you can do to stay safe are actually very easy. First, *tell someone where you are going, whom you're going with, and what time you'll be back.* Adults forget to do this as often as kids do. But how are you going to be found if no one knows where you went? Rescuers could spend hours or even days looking for you in all the wrong places. So remember: the best way to make sure that you are found is to make sure that somebody knows where you might be lost.

Another great thing you can do is to *take friends along with you.* Having one or more buddies along makes good sense for lots of reasons. For starters, it's much easier to find a group of people than it is to find just one. Also, friends can help you build a shelter, collect water, and make noise so that people can find you. And being lost is less scary when you are not alone. Your buddy doesn't even have to be a person—you can bring a dog friend with you to keep you company and keep you warm. If you are with another person or a group of people, stay together.

Last, *always carry water, food, and a survival kit.* Your kit can be as simple as a water bottle and purification tablets, a lighter, a candy bar, a flashlight, toilet paper, some garbage bags, a first-aid kit, and a whistle. You can read more about more advanced survival kits in chapter 12 (p. 191).

Just by doing these three things—letting someone know where you're going, taking a buddy along, and having a survival kit with you—you'll know that you've done the most important things you can to make sure that you'll be found alive and well. But what is better than being found alive and well? Not getting lost in the first place, of course. So how can you help to make sure you don't get lost? Let's look at some of the most common reasons that people (adults as well as kids) find themselves lost in the wilderness:

- **It gets too dark to see where you're going.**
  It's easy to misjudge distances or lose track of time
  when you are exploring and enjoying the outdoors,
  and activities such as day hikes and rafting trips
  frequently last longer than expected. Out in the
  wilderness, especially in the mountains, it can get
  dark quickly: all of a sudden, the sun disappears
  behind a hill and you realize you have a long way
  to walk in the dark to return to your camp or car.
  Always carry a flashlight or headlamp, as well as
  extra batteries, with you when you head out into
  the wilderness.

- **Someone gets hurt.** It's easy to twist an ankle or
  stumble and fall when hiking, and you can get sick
  out in the woods just as easily as you can at home.
  If you or someone you're with is hurt or ill—even if
  that someone is your dog—you may not be able to
  make it back to civilization before nightfall. Be sure
  to bring along basic first-aid and signaling tools
  whenever you go on hikes or other wilderness
  excursions. That way, you'll be prepared for
  emergencies and you'll be easier to find if you have
  to be rescued.

- **The weather changes suddenly.** I live in the
  mountains, where it snows at unexpected times, even
  in the middle of summer. In both mountains and
  deserts, fierce rainstorms can occur with very little
  warning and make rocks and trails slippery. In

many areas of the country it can become foggy, making it difficult to see or stay on trails. Oftentimes it is more dangerous to try to walk through bad weather than it is to sit tight and wait it out. If you have your survival pack with you, you can make a raincoat out of a garbage bag and build a fire to keep you warm as you wait for the weather to clear.

- **You take a "shortcut" that turns out to be a mistake.** When you are tired and on a switchback trail—one that zigzags up a steep hill—it may seem like you can save time by going straight up the hill instead. But once you leave a trail it can be surprisingly hard to find your way back to it. Hike only on marked trails and avoid shortcuts that lead you off them.

- **You follow a false trail.** Well-worn animal paths often look like trails made by and for humans. It's easy to veer off onto an animal trail by mistake and be unable to find your way back to the "people path." How can you make sure that you stay on track? One way is to mark your trail as you hike into the wilderness so you can follow your markings when you hike back out. To show where you've been, you can put a small rock on top of a big rock or place two sticks together on the trail so that they point like an arrow to show your direction. You can also tie brightly colored flagging tape (which can be bought at most hardware and outdoor equipment stores) to branches or rocks to mark your path. The test is to look back and make sure that you can always spot the last marking as you go along; that way, you'll know that you will be able to spot them when you return along the trail. If you use flagging tape, be sure to remove it as you walk back. No one wants a messy forest.

- **The trail is rocky and there aren't any footprints to help you stay on the path.** How can you tell that you haven't veered off the trail if you have to travel over rocks? Some trails are marked with "ducks," which are little piles of rocks that show you where the trail is. One rock on top of another means "go straight ahead," a small rock to the right of a big rock means "turn right," and a little rock to the left of a big rock means "turn left." If a rocky trail isn't marked, you can make your own ducks, tie some flagging tape to a rock, or mark your way with branch arrows.

- **You go exploring and end up in a place that is totally unfamiliar to you.** As you go along, try to

pick out landmarks that you can look for when
you head back. Of course, if you bring a GPS (Global
Positioning System) with you, you'll always be able to
tell where you are. (See chapter 10, p. 172, for
information on navigating via GPS.)

- **You have to leave the trail in order to get
  around something that's in the way.** In the
  spring, streams of rainwater or melted snow may
  block sections of a trail. Big trees and boulders may
  fall across the path. If you have to leave the trail to
  get around an obstacle such as these, you could
  wind up off track. Pay attention to what your trail
  looks like, and when you get back to it on the other
  side of the obstacle, make sure it looks the same. You
  don't want to end up on an animal track or a different
  trail by mistake.

- **You leave the trail to go swimming, fishing,
  or exploring.** Everyone has left a trail to watch
  wildlife, go fishing, or investigate something
  interesting. If you do, keep track of the path you take,
  and be sure to return to the trail the same way you
  left it.

- **You become dehydrated.** When you are exercising
  and you don't drink enough fluids, you can quickly
  become *dehydrated*, which means your body has
  lost too much water to stay healthy. This happens
  most frequently in hot or even warm weather, but it
  can happen at any time. Dehydration can make you

too weak and sick to get back home on your own. To prevent this, bring extra water and don't forget to drink it.

- **You deliberately go off on your own.** Kids sometimes get mad at their parents, a brother or sister, or a friend and just take off without paying attention to where they're going.

The secret to being a smart adventurer is to be prepared for any of these possibilities and to know how to take care of yourself if something unexpected happens.

WHAT TO DO IF YOU GET LOST

Realizing you are lost is a really scary feeling, and most people make it worse by becoming angry, frightened, sad, or ashamed instead of taking control of the situation. Your biggest survival tool is your brain. So stop blaming yourself or others and don't waste valuable time. Stay calm. You will be found—probably soon. You *are* going to survive, and you need to get to work to make your situation better. Remember, your main job now is to stay healthy and protected until you are located. If you find yourself panicking or running in circles, just take a deep breath and say to yourself, "STOP":

- **S is for Stop.** If there are many hours left before sunset and you can clearly see your tracks, just follow them back to safety.

But if you don't have enough time to get back before sunset or if you have no idea how to get back, *stop moving*. The more you move around, the longer it will take others to find you. Also, *stop panicking*. It is normal to be scared and upset, but you are the only one who can make things better, so stay calm. Remember that you know how to make a shelter and take care of yourself. Tell yourself that you will be OK until you really believe it, even if you have to say it a hundred times. You *will* make it. You are a survivor!

- **T is for Think**. After you take a couple of deep breaths, start thinking. Who knows where you are? What's around you that can make your situation better? Is there something in your pack or pockets that will help? How many hours are left until dark? Are you in a good spot to set up a shelter? What is the weather like? What kind of shelter can you build?

- **O is for Observe**. Look around you. Is there a meadow with high grass nearby? Meadow grass makes soft bedding. Is there a lot of snow? Maybe you can dig into a snowbank to make a snow cave. Listen and look for water; you will need it to survive. Also look for a wide-open spot that you can use to signal for help.

- **P is for Plan**. Decide what to do, and in what order. What do you need to do first?

Are you in a safe spot? If there is a thunderstorm and you're high up on a mountain or hill, you need to get to lower ground as soon as you can. Be sure to stay away from big boulders and tall trees that are standing by themselves—lightning is most likely to strike there.

Do you need to build a shelter to help protect yourself from bad weather? Do you need to make a fire to stay warm? If so, these tasks should be at or near the top of your "to do" list. Plan where you will look for shelter-building materials and firewood. (You always need more firewood than you expect, so plan to collect more than you think you will need.)

Do you have water? Finding a supply is also important, if you have forgotten to bring extra and the weather is hot. However, do not wander around looking for water, especially if you know someone will be coming to find you.

What can you do to help people find you? Is there an open space where you can signal an airplane or helicopter? Can you build a signal fire safely, or are you surrounded by flammable grass? Are there rocks that you can use to make an X in the snow or in a field?

HELP IS ON THE WAY

If you go missing, the first thing your parents or guardians will probably do is notify the police or a park ranger. These officials will call in a SAR, or search and rescue, team. These dedicated searchers help to find kids and adults

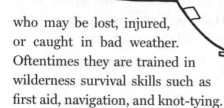

who may be lost, injured,
or caught in bad weather.
Oftentimes they are trained in
wilderness survival skills such as
first aid, navigation, and knot-tying.

Search and rescue teams may
include park rangers, deputy sheriffs, and
volunteers who live in the area. Some team members work
as "ground pounders," who travel on foot to find lost people, while others serve as ATV (all-terrain vehicle) drivers,
searching back roads and trails. Mounted searchers ride
horses that have been specially trained to work with search
dogs and to not be spooked by things like ATVs, chainsaws,
tents, sirens, helicopters, or blowing flagging tape. And
search and rescue pilots may fly helicopters and airplanes
in order to search from the sky.

Essential to search and rescue are K-9 teams made
up of search dogs and their handlers. The dogs can smell
people from far away, and they can follow the scent trails
people leave behind as they walk. Search dogs are trained
to ride in helicopters and ATVs, to be obedient, and to
follow instructions well. In addition, they are usually
excellent swimmers. A search dog may be any breed, but
all search dogs have two things in common: they are eager
to work and they love to find people.

There are two kinds of search dogs. *Area search dogs* run free and look for any human who's nearby. If they find someone, they run back to their handlers and tell them by barking or jumping up on their human partners. Then they bring them to the lost person. *Trailing dogs* work on long leashes that are held by their handlers. Usually the handlers allow the trailing dogs to smell something that has the lost person's scent on it, such as a sweater or other piece of clothing. (Every person on the planet has a different smell. Even twins smell different to a search dog.) Then, ignoring hundreds of other smells, the trailing dogs follow that unique scent into the wilderness until they reach the source of the smell—the lost person.

Most dogs that work in search and rescue wear orange vests, called *shabracks*, that identify them as working dogs. Also, most of these dogs wear bells on their harness. The bells help the handlers keep track of the dogs, and they help lost people to know that help is nearby. If you are lost and you hear bells, start yelling or blowing your whistle to help the search teams find you.

If they are called in to help find you, search and rescue people will grab their search packs, load up their horses, dogs, and ATVs, and report to the search headquarters, which is called the command post. Your parent or guardian will be asked many questions, such as what you look like, how old you are, what you are wearing, and whether or not you have any survival training. They may be asked for a piece of clothing or some other item that has your scent on it so that the dogs on the search and rescue team can learn your smell. Pilots might fly planes or helicopters over the area where you went missing. That location is called PLS, "place last seen" (or "point last seen"). If there are danger-ous weather conditions and it is dark, the searchers may not be allowed to search until daybreak or until conditions improve. That is why it is important for you to be able to take care of yourself for a few hours or a day until they find you. Remember, people *are* coming to find you, as soon as they can.

What if *you're* not lost, but someone that you are with, like a little brother or sister, wanders away from you and goes missing as you are exploring the wilderness together?

What do you do? You can be a big help to search and rescue by marking the spot where you last saw that person. Perhaps you could make a big X on the trail with sticks. Then go get help from an adult.

Lots of kids who are lost do something that could prevent them from being rescued: they hide from the people who are searching for them, either because their parents told them not to speak to strangers or because they think that people will be angry with them for getting lost. There have been cases where, for several days, searchers were just a few feet away from the lost kids they were looking for, but the cold and hungry children stayed hidden in the bushes because they were afraid of what would happen to them when they were found. This kind of behavior is dangerous and it isn't very smart. Search and rescue people not only risk their own lives to find lost kids, but they often put their horses and dogs in danger, too. Don't be one of those kids who hide from the people who are trying to save them. Your parents want you to be found. Just ask them.

BUILDING A SHELTER

If you're lost and working out the steps in your survival plan, you'll need to keep in mind the *rule of three*, which states that you can live about three weeks without food and three days without water, but only three hours without adequate shelter if the weather is extreme (and only three minutes without air). This means that building a shelter is one of the first survival skills you'll put to use. And since most people discover they are lost late in the afternoon, you'll probably need to work quickly to finish your shelter before dark. Even if you aren't lost but are just out camping or adventuring, the same rule applies: build your shelter first.

A shelter can help to keep you warm when it's cold outside and cool when it's hot. It can protect you from rain, snow, and other bad weather conditions. And it can give you a more comfortable place to sleep. There are many different types of shelters, and the kind you should build will depend on the weather, what materials are nearby, and what tools you have. And, of course, before you can build your shelter, you have to decide where to build it.

CHOOSING A LOCATION

It's important to think carefully about the best place to build your shelter. If you're worried about the cold, pick a spot halfway up a hill, preferably on a sunny slope—that's where it'll be warmest. Camping next to a big rock that has sat in the sun all day will also help keep you warm. To escape the heat, choose a place near water, if you can—it can be as much as 10 to 15 degrees cooler there than it is up on a hill. That temperature difference could save your life. However, if you stay next to the water, expect company. During warm months, bees, mosquitoes, and flies like to hang out near water. Also, be aware that some streams and rivers can rise several feet overnight. To be on the safe side, build your shelter at a spot about 10 feet higher than the waterline (10 feet is the height of a basketball hoop). Otherwise, you might find yourself swimming in your sleep!

If you are in the desert, you should never camp at the bottom of a canyon or a dry riverbed, which is often called a *wash* or an *arroyo*, because rainwater from miles away can pour down canyon walls and create dangerous flash floods without warning. I have seen giant boulders get washed down normally dry canyons after summer thunderstorms, even though the canyons were nearly a mile away from where it was actually raining.

Try to pick a location that's close to a trail so rescuers or hikers can find you quickly. But don't build your shelter in the middle of a trail or directly next to one. Deer, skunks, mountain lions, bobcats, coyotes, and bears often walk down trails at night, especially if those trails lead to water, and you don't want to have to deal with any unexpected visitors in the middle of the night. Move off the trail a bit, then look for a safe spot to build your shelter.

How can you tell whether a particular spot is safe? First, make sure you're protected if a strong wind blows through—you want to avoid big trees with dead branches that might fall on you. Then, check for any trees nearby that have been struck by lightning; that can mean you are in a lightning danger zone. (People commonly say that lightning doesn't strike twice in the same place, but that is totally untrue. In fact, lightning has been known to strike the same object multiple times during one storm.) And remember, you will usually be protected from lightning strikes if you stay away from mountaintops, high rocks, open spaces, or lone trees. Keep low and stay out of water during thunderstorms.

In addition, make sure you're not choosing a spot that's already been claimed by tiny biting creatures like ticks or ants. I once started to build a shelter, only to discover a gigantic anthill under the pine needles where I was making my bed. Kick away any needles and leaves and look around for anthills, scorpion holes, spiderwebs, and anything else that may mean unwanted company in your temporary home. It's also a good idea to avoid setting up your shelter next to big piles of rocks, as venomous snakes sometimes live under them during the day and then come out at night to hunt. Snakes do not usually travel long distances, so if you see a suspicious-looking rock pile or a venomous snake, just build your shelter about 100 yards away from it. One hundred yards is the length of a football field.

Finally, make sure that there are enough materials nearby with which to build a shelter. (See the building instructions later in the chapter to find out what you'll need.) If one spot doesn't have enough building materials, move to a spot that has more. You don't want to have to spend a lot of time and energy hauling shelter materials a long way, especially if you make your shelter halfway up a hill, where it is warmer.

ACTIVITY The next time you go for a walk in the woods or the desert, look around you. What do you see that you could use for shelter materials?

How long will it take to make your shelter? Most of the time, it takes at least an hour and a half to find materials and build a shelter. Of course, you want to have it all built before it gets really dark. But how can you tell when the sun will set? Just use your hand. Hold your arm straight out in front with your palm facing you and your fingers together. Line up your pinky with the horizon. The space that's taken up by your four fingers counts as one hour, and the space of one finger counts as 15 minutes. Count how many "hands" and "fingers" it is between the horizon and the sun, and that's how long it is until sunset.

ABOUT TWO HOURS BEFORE SUNSET

What should you do if you have no time to build a shelter? See the section on natural shelters on p. 24.

BASIC RULES FOR SHELTER BUILDING

Once you've chosen the site for your shelter, the next step is to plan the size of your bed. Be sure to do this before you construct the shelter walls. There is nothing more annoying than spending a lot of energy to create a warm shelter, only to find out that you don't fit inside! Your shelter should be just large enough to lie down in. The smaller it is, the better it will help to keep you warm by trapping your body heat. Smaller shelters also require less work to build than larger ones.

Never sleep on the bare ground in cold weather. Cold ground will pull your body heat right out of you. A layer of natural bedding materials will insulate you from the ground. The best bedding materials are dried grasses, but you can also use pine needles, pine boughs, tiny pine cones, or leaves. If you are in an area with few soft bedding materials, save the softest materials for the top: use pine boughs, leaves, or tiny pinecones as the bottom layer, then cover the top with the fluffiest leaves, grasses, or pine needles. The thicker the bed, the warmer it will be. In fact, make your bed twice as thick as you think it has to be. During the night, those leaves and grasses will smash down and compress. If it is raining, dig a small ditch around your shelter to drain the water away so it doesn't flow into your bed.

As you'll learn in chapter 12 (p. 191), your survival kit should contain at least two large plastic trash bags. They're handy for many purposes, especially when you're building a shelter. They're great for hauling shelter materials, and you can fill them with leaves or needles to make a mattress or a blanket. They can even become a waterproof part of the shelter itself.

KNOTS

In order to build a shelter or perform a number of other survival tasks, it helps to know how to tie knots. Although there are literally hundreds of different knots, you only need to learn a few of them. Basic knots such as the bowline are useful for tying your shelter's central support to a tree or hanging your food stash out of the reach of bears. They are simple to learn and can be untied easily so you can reuse your rope. Knot-tying is difficult to describe, but many websites have animated instructions to help you learn. (See the resources section, p. 207.) The best way to learn knots, however, is to watch others tie them and then practice with your own rope; you can receive hands-on training from the Boy Scouts or Girl Scouts, rock climbing schools, and some sporting good stores.

- **Bowline.** This is the most basic knot. It is primarily used to attach a single rope to something like a tree, and it is easy to tie and untie—except when the rope is stretched taut by some kind of weight (like a backpack hanging from it). To tie a bowline, make a small loop in the rope. Bring the end of the rope up through the loop, around the rope, and back down into the loop. Pull tight.

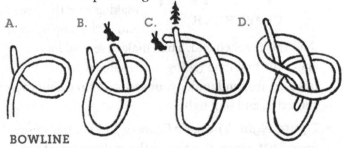

BOWLINE

A. **Make a rabbit hole**

B. **The rabbit pops out of the hole**

C. **The rabbit runs around the tree**

D. **And the rabbit hops back into the hole**

- **Clove hitch.** A clove hitch is used to tie something like a tarp to a pole. It is useful because you can adjust your rope length as you tie it, which is important when tying a tarp tightly to a stake or stringing a light food bag up in the air. However, it is not the strongest knot, and it should not be used for heavy jobs like stringing a hammock between trees—it could loosen under pressure and dump you to the ground. To use a clove hitch, first attach the object that needs fastening (food bag, tarp, etc.) to

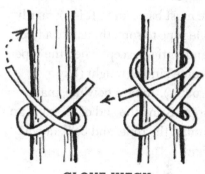

CLOVE HITCH

one end of the rope using a bowline or other secure knot, and then loop the opposite end of the rope around the object to which you're attaching it (post, stake, etc.), making sure the free end of the loop is lower than the attached end. Then make a second loop above the first loop (going in the same direction), poke the free end under your second loop where you started it, and pull tight.

- **Figure eight.** The basic figure eight knot is a *stopper knot.* That means it is tied at the end of a rope to keep it from sliding through a hole. It can also be used as a basic knot; it is stronger and more secure than a

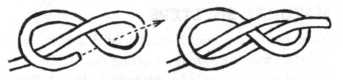

FIGURE EIGHT

bowline and can hold a heavy weight. Form a loop near one end of the rope, pass the loose end back over the top of your loop and poke the end through the first loop, then tighten it. If you do it correctly, it should look like the number 8.

- **Double figure eight**. The double figure eight knot is used to link two ropes together (the ropes do not need to be the same size). First, make a basic figure eight knot. To add another rope, just follow the path of the original figure eight knot with the new rope. Start it where the first knot ends and keep the new rope neat and side by side with the original.

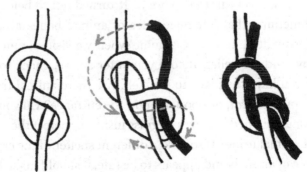

DOUBLE FIGURE EIGHT

NATURAL SHELTERS

If you don't have enough time to build a shelter before nightfall, find a naturally occurring one. If you're in a wooded area, you might be able to find a large hollow log that you can climb into; you can cover the entrance with leaves or other materials to keep out the cold. Logs often have bee or wasp nests in them, so be sure to check for prior residents before climbing inside. If there are no logs around, you can burrow into a big pile of leaves or pine needles and cover yourself as much as possible. If you find a depression or a hole in the ground, you can build a shelter by covering the top with branches, small logs, and leaves.

Some areas of the country have caves or rock overhangs that can protect you from snow or rain. However you must first make sure that you are not sharing your space with an animal. When I was young, my brother and I found a cave and went in to explore it. It turned out to belong to something that left huge piles of animal bones around. Fortunately, no one was home when we visited, much to my mother's relief. Before you enter a cave, check to see if you have the place to yourself. Are there animal tracks or piles of *scat*, or poop, around the entrance? Do you see bones or a bed of leaves or grass inside, or detect the smell of animal urine? If so, find a different shelter. If the cave is free of animals and appears to be safe, it should make for a really good shelter.

> ❌ *Never build a fire in a cave or under a rock overhang.* Rocks in overhangs or in the ceilings of caves sometimes break off and fall when heated. If you build a fire (see chapter 5 for instructions), put it just outside the cave or overhang.

In many states, explorers may come across abandoned mines. *Stay out of them!* There are gases inside mines that can kill you if you breathe the air. Rattlesnakes, scorpions, and mountain lions like to live in them. And mines are unstable; many have floors that could fall out from under you and roofs that could cave in. There may be old—but still dangerous—explosives nearby, as well. Mines are especially common in the Southwest, along the West Coast, and in Michigan, Alaska, Idaho, Montana, Wyoming, and Utah. There are over a half-million abandoned mine openings in the United States. Some mines are easy to spot because they have wooden beams around their entrances, railroad tracks leading into them, or old mining equipment and buildings nearby. There may be fences or barbed wire around them to keep people away. But some mines don't have any of these features, and their openings might look just like a hole in the ground or in the side of a hill.

TARP SHELTERS

A tarp shelter is a good choice when you're in a warm climate and you either want some shade or want to protect yourself from rain. If you don't have a real tarp, you can use a trash bag, cut open on the long side to make one large plastic sheet. There are several ways to build a tarp shelter, depending on the size of your tarp and the materials, such as rocks, trees, or bushes, that are available to use as anchors:

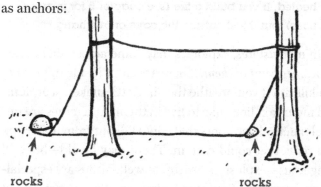

rocks   rocks

- You can use a clove hitch knot to tie the top corners of a tarp to two trees or two bushes so that the tarp is stretched between them. Pull the bottom edge of the tarp out and down to make sort of a half tent, and use something heavy, such as sand, rocks, or logs, to hold each of the bottom corners in place.

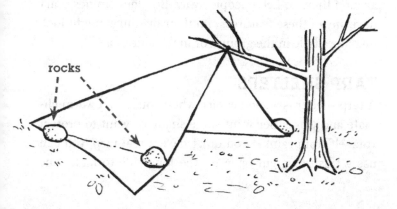

rocks

- You can fold the tarp on the diagonal, tie one corner of your fold to an overhanging branch using a bowline knot, and hold all the edges down with rocks to make an open-ended tent.

- If you have a tube tent in your survival kit, you can create a tarp shelter quickly. A tube tent is an open-ended plastic tent that comes with a rope and is small enough to carry in your pocket.

TRENCH SHELTERS

A trench shelter is a basic shelter that will protect you from both heat and cold. You can build it in areas where there is snow or sand on the ground that can be dug into easily by hand. It can also be built in wooded areas where the roots of fallen trees have left pits in the ground. Just follow these instructions:

1. Dig out a pit, piling the snow, soft dirt, or sand around the edges to make it deeper. Remember, the pit should be just large enough for you to lie down comfortably, just beneath the pit edges you created. Leave an opening at one end so you can slide down into your shelter.

2. Make your bed at the bottom of the pit. Be sure to line it with lots of pine branches, bark, or leaves to keep you off the wet ground.

3. Lay sticks and branches across the top to form a roof. Then put a tarp or garbage bag over it.

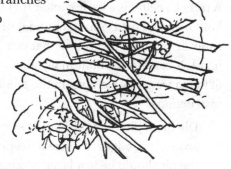

4. Cover the top of your stick roof with layers of bark, branches, leaves, pine needles, driftwood, dried seaweed, snow, or whatever you have available to seal it.

5. Slide into the trench, feet first, and close off your entrance, leaving open a small hole for fresh air.

BRUSH SHELTERS

A brush shelter is another type of shelter that can be constructed easily and quickly in most environments. You don't have to dig into the ground or use much energy to build it—as long as you have enough building materials nearby. Two girls in my neighborhood built a demonstration brush shelter in an hour. They had no ax or tools, yet they were able to create a warm, waterproof place to sleep in a short period of time. Here is how you can build one:

1. Find a sturdy dead tree to serve as your shelter's central support, or *ridgepole*. It needs to be strong enough to use as a backbone for your shelter, at least three or four feet longer than your body length, and small enough to lift and move. Break off any sharp branches that are sticking out along it.

2. Pick someplace secure to prop up your ridgepole—a sturdy, somewhat flat spot about four feet off the ground. The spot can be the place on a tree where two branches come together, or a small boulder. Lay the narrower end of your ridgepole against the flat spot and drop the wider end onto the ground. If you have cord or a shoelace, you can give your shelter more stability by tying the top of

your ridgepole tightly to a tree, large rock, or other secure object, using a secure knot such as a bowline.

3. Gather bedding materials and carry them to your shelter. (Remember, you can carry them in a trash bag.)

4. Make your bed under the ridgepole, stretch out on it, and make sure you fit inside. Adjust the ridgepole if necessary.

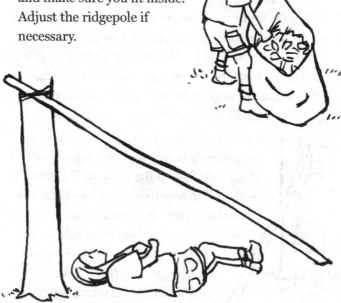

5. Drape a tarp over your ridgepole to make a tent and secure each side of it to the ground with rocks, branches, or other materials. If you have no tarp, cut along the long edge of some trash bags, open them up, and use them instead. (You can use duct tape to attach two trash bags to each other to make one large sheet of plastic.) Once the tarp or bag is in place, prop branches and sticks from the ground to the ridgepole to make a tent-shaped frame. If you only have a small tarp or trash bag that doesn't reach the ground when you drape it over the ridgepole, build the basic stick frame first, then drape the tarp over the top of it.

6. Fill in the frame with more sticks, branches, or large slabs of bark. Weave in smaller branches to hold everything together, and stuff bark, leaves, and other materials into the walls until every part of the shelter

is covered except the entrance. If you have fresh pine or cedar branches, layer them on top to make your roof somewhat waterproof. The thicker the shelter—the more materials in the walls—the warmer it will be.

7. Make a shelter door. You can use your backpack, a garbage bag full of leaves, or a pile of branches to close off the entrance, or you can just pull your tarp closed.

ACTIVITY The only way you will ever find out what makes for a great shelter is to build one and test it out. Make a brush shelter according to the instructions above, then try spending the night inside to see how comfortable it is. Does it keep you warm? Does it keep you dry when it's raining? It's fun to build survival shelters—and, with practice, you will get better and better at making them.

BEACH SHELTERS

Many beaches are covered with driftwood and logs. These are great materials for building a temporary home. Don't forget to make your shelter above the high-tide line—the spot to which the water rises to when it's at its highest—or you might find yourself washed away in the middle of the night. To locate the high-tide line on an open beach, look for the water mark that's farthest from the water; it often is edged with driftwood and debris.

If you're lost or stranded on a beach, the best shelter you can build is a trench shelter (see p. 27). Dig a trench that's big enough to comfortably lie down in, and pile your dugout sand around the edges, leaving an entrance to get in and out. Line the trench with grasses or dried seaweed. Make a roof by laying driftwood across the top of the trench, biggest pieces first, and then covering it completely with stacks of wood. You could also make a tarp shelter (see p. 25), but that will not keep you very warm at night, so you may also need to make a fire (see "Building a Fire," p. 59).

SNOW SHELTERS

Snow shelters have saved many people, especially lost skiers. Just one candle can keep the temperature inside a snow shelter at about 32 degrees even when it is much colder outside. Snow is a great *insulator*, which means that it keeps out the wind and cold. In a snow shelter with a thick layer of branches or leaves for a bed, you can survive terrible conditions.

If you happen to find a big, packed-down mound of snow that's not too hard to dig into, you can carve out a small cave with your gloved hands or a piece of wood, as shown in the illustration below. The cave should be a bit longer than your body and tall enough to sit up in. Inside, scrape off the snow above you to make a domed roof. The area for your bed should be at least six inches higher than the entrance—the higher the better, because then the cold air will sink below your sleeping platform and keep you warmer. It is important to poke a tennis ball-sized hole through the roof of your snow cave in order to allow oxygen to get inside. You can do this with a long stick. Be sure to keep the stick with you inside the shelter to keep the hole open or make a new one if necessary. *Never close yourself inside any snow shel-ter that does not have an air hole.*

stick for air hole

cold air collects here

Unfortunately, you may not be able to find the kind of snow that's needed to build a snow cave. I lived in snow country for years, but most of the snow I saw was either too light and powdery or hard as a rock. But there is another way to make a good snow shelter. In the western mountains you can often find spruce or cedar trees with branches that touch the ground. What little snow there is under these trees is usually soft and easy to dig—perfect for making a trench shelter (see p. 27). Simply scoop out a hole in the snow next to the tree, pile the scooped-out snow around the top of the hole—leaving an opening to climb in and out—and make a roof out of sticks and boughs. You can then cover the entire roof with snow to insulate it. Like all snow shelters, the smaller the warmer—make it just taller than your head when sitting down. Don't forget to line the bottom of your trench with a thick layer of branches so you are not lying on the cold ground or in the snow.

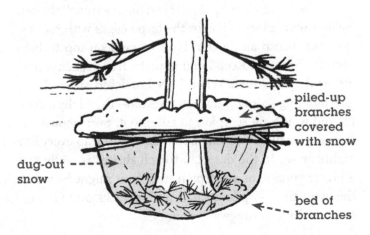

piled-up
branches
covered
with snow

dug-out
snow

bed of
branches

DESERT SHELTERS

People who walk or drive through the desert during daylight hours can go for miles without ever seeing a single animal. That doesn't mean they're not there, though. In hot climates, most creatures are *nocturnal*—active at night—and they spend their days sleeping in holes they've dug deep underground, where it is cool. Desert animals such as coyotes, skunks, snakes, and mice know how to survive when the ground is hot enough to burn bare feet.

If you're lost in the desert, a top priority will be to build a shelter that helps you to stay cool and protected from the sun. But it can get very cold in the desert once the sun goes down, so you'll also need it to keep you warm at night. The kind of desert shelter you can build depends totally on the materials you have around you and with you. A tarp or extra-large garbage bag can be used to make a simple tarp shelter for shade (see p. 25), or you can build a trench shelter in the sand (see p. 27). If you make a trench shelter, cover it with a tarp—anchor the tarp's edges with rocks—then pile brush and a thin layer of sand on top to help keep the heat out. Keep in mind that a trench shelter may attract desert critters. When I lived in desert states, I saw kids building scorpion traps in the sand—they'd dig a deep pit and wait for a scorpion to fall into it. Sure enough, at least one or two scorpions would fall into a trap every few nights or so. In the desert, a trench shelter is really just a bigger version of a scorpion trap, so it might be worth the extra time to pile a small wall of rocks around your entrance to discourage any visitors.

If you are stranded in a car in the desert and there is no other shade, you can dig under the car and make a cool place to rest until it cools off at night.

CARS

Sometimes families get lost or stranded while driving in an unfamiliar wilderness area. The most important thing to remember is to *stay with your car* unless there is a very good reason to leave. Your car provides better shelter than anything you could construct. It protects you from dangerous predators, snakes, and insects. It is much easier to spot a car from the air than it is to spot a person. There is gas in the tank for starting fires, and there might be tools, extra clothing, and perhaps a blanket in the trunk. (In fact, every family should carry an emergency kit in their car. See chapter 12, p. 204, for more information on what it should include.)

3

FINDING WATER

Think back to the rule of three, discussed in the previous chapter (p. 15). It states that you can survive for only about three hours without shelter in extreme weather—but also that you can't go without water for more than three days. Obviously, in a survival situation, water is another of your most urgent needs.

To stay healthy, you need at least two to three quarts (64 to 96 ounces) of water a day. If you are exercising or doing physical labor, if you are sick, or if you're outside in hot or cold weather, you will need lots more. A big, two-liter plastic soda bottle holds about 66 ounces of fluid; that's the *minimum* amount of water you need to drink every day. Whenever you head out to hike or explore the wilderness, be sure that you bring along plenty of water: two full 32-ounce bottles. You can buy 32-ounce hard plastic water bottles at camping and sporting goods stores. If you get lost, you'll know that you need to drink at least those two bottles' worth of water every day to stay healthy.

If you're lost and your water supply is running out, look for another source of fresh water (see "How to Locate Water," p. 41)—but remember, don't stray too far or rescuers will have trouble finding you. Most river and lake water is not safe to drink untreated, but you can purify it (see "Water Purification," p. 45). If you have a freshwater source, drink, drink, drink whenever you need to.

> ❌ **No matter how thirsty you are, *do not drink water from the ocean or any other source of salt water*. Ocean water has so much salt in it that your body will flush extra water out of it trying to wash out the salt. You'll end up with less water in your body than you started with.**

Your body is telling you that you need water when your mouth is dry and sticky and you feel thirsty. You may also feel sick to your stomach, weak, tired, or dizzy, or you may get a bad headache. Check the color of your pee as well: if it's dark yellow, you need to drink more water.

If you have little or no water and you don't think that you will be able to find any, do not go running around. Rest. Better yet, rest in the shade. And keep your head covered if possible. You don't want to get dehydrated.

What exactly is dehydration? It happens when you don't have enough water in your body and you are losing more water than you are taking in. Even mild dehydration can make you tired, give you headaches, and make it difficult to think. You can get dehydrated if you don't drink enough water, if you sweat a lot (either from physical activity or because it's hot outside), or if you're throwing up or you have diarrhea. People frequently become dehydrated during hot weather, but you can just as easily get dehydrated on a cold and wintry day or night. Be sure to drink plenty of water in the wintertime—not only will you avoid dehydration, but also the more water you have in your system, the better your blood circulates and the warmer you will be.

HOW TO LOCATE WATER

The cleanest natural sources of fresh water are springs (sources of water that come up from the ground), snow, and tiny, fast-flowing streams. Lakes and ponds come next; then come all other wet and marshy areas (except for oceans and other saltwater areas, which should *never* be used as a water source).

The lower in elevation you are, the more likely the water is contaminated with things that can make you sick. However, the lower you go, the more likely you are to find water. Experts believe that the most harmful microscopic bugs in water live near the surface, so try to collect water from the *bottom* of a stream or lake, by covering your water bottle's opening with your hand and sticking it deeper into the water before taking your hand away.

What is safer—a pond with green algae around the edges and water bugs swimming in it, or a clear pond with no green algae or bugs? In some areas, the pond with bugs in it might be safer. There are many places where chemicals come from the soil and make the water poisonous. Bugs are often a sign that the water may be safe.

Other sources of water include dry riverbeds, where you can sometimes find water below the surface if you dig down a foot or two, especially if you dig under an overhanging bank. You can also check for water at the bottom of a rocky hill; if it has rained recently, water might have collected there. Or you can look for damp areas where green plants are growing together in thick groups.

Certain plants only grow where there is water. In dry areas, cottonwood trees and desert willows usually only grow where there is underground water. Cottonwoods are large trees with rough bark and bright green leaves in the spring and summer. Desert willows are big trees that

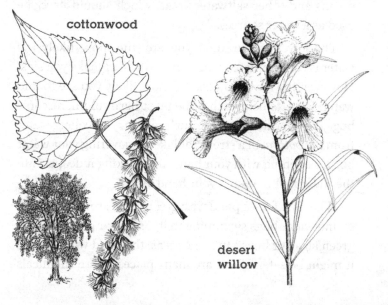

cottonwood

desert willow

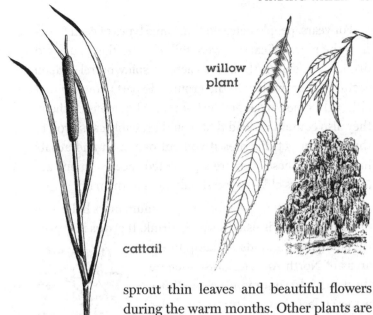

willow
plant

cattail

sprout thin leaves and beautiful flowers
during the warm months. Other plants are
usually found growing in water or in damp
soil, including cattails and willow plants. Cattails are tall
plants with long, grassy leaves and brown, hot-dog-shaped
spikes. Willow plants are green shrubs covered with nar-
row green leaves; in the spring they grow *catkins*, which
are fuzzy seedpods that feel like cat fur.

You will find more flying insects when you are near water. Dragonflies, especially, are never far from water. Birds
fly to water in the morning and evening as well. Of course,
all kinds of animals have to seek out water at some point. If
you find an animal trail next to your water source, you need
to be especially careful to purify the water, because many
animals contaminate water with feces (poop) or urine.

For years, people believed that some types of cacti ("cacti" is the plural of cactus) were full of water that you could drink—particularly the barrel cactus, a spiky, barrel-shaped cactus that grows low to the ground. Experts now say that although some barrel cacti do hold some liquid inside them, they also contain an acid that would probably cause you to throw up or get diarrhea if you cut one open and ate its insides. And these cacti are a protected species—many are 50 to 130 years old—so you should not cut them up.

If you are lost in a wet forest, sphagnum moss holds lots of rainwater that is usually safe to drink. It grows in greenish clumps or mounds in damp forest areas of North America. Just squeeze the water into your mouth. Sometimes water collects in tree stumps, in holes in trees, or in the leaves of plants. Rainwater is safe to drink without purifying it, as long as it is collected in a clean container like a tarp.

sphagnum moss

So is most snow. It's always best to melt snow and then drink the water; if you eat unmelted snow, your body temperature will be lowered much faster. Snow can be melted by placing it in a water bottle and putting the bottle inside your clothes. (Don't put it next to your skin, because it can lower your body temperature.) Or, if the weather is warm enough, you can pack a bottle with snow and set it in the sun. Do not eat unmelted snow unless you have no other choice.

WATER PURIFICATION

In most areas of the country there are tiny creatures living in rivers, lakes, and streams. They are so small that they can only be seen through a microscope, but they can make you very ill. Cryptosporidium and giardia are two of the most common types. You generally will not feel sick right away, but symptoms will start to show after about a week. To be safe, you should purify any water you collect from rivers, lakes, and streams before you drink it.

However, because you can't go without water for very long, if you need to drink, do it, even if you can't disinfect the water. You will die of dehydration faster than you would from any germs in the water. You can always see a doctor after you are rescued.

There are many different ways to make water safe to drink. The easiest way is to use water purification tablets. They are made of iodine or chlorine and they take up almost no room in your pack. You fill your 32-ounce bottle with water, drop in one tablet, shake, and wait for anywhere from one to four hours, depending on the type of tablet, and presto—you have clean water. A couple of times while you are disinfecting your water, loosen the top of your water bottle and shake the bottle gently to disinfect the bottle's lip. The iodine tablets work especially well, but water that's been purified with iodine doesn't taste very good. Most people who use iodine tablets also carry packets of powdered vitamin C drink mix to put into their iodine-treated water after it's purified to make it taste better.

Always carry iodine or chlorine tablets with you when you're out hiking or exploring.

Or you can buy water purification devices with special filters that clean the water in a bottle or allow you to sip it through a straw. There are even battery-powered ultraviolet (UV) lights that kill viruses, germs, and parasites—you just stick them into your bottle of water and turn them on. No matter what type of purification device you choose, be sure you know how to use it before you head out into the wilderness.

If, for some reason, you don't have a purification device, you can boil your water to kill the germs and microscopic creatures that can make you sick. People have been using this method to make water safe to drink for years and years. If you have a container and a fire you can heat up dry stones to bring the water in the cup to a boil. (Chapter 5, p. 59, shows you how to build a fire.) *Do not* use rocks that have been sitting in water or that have holes in them where water could collect, as they can explode when heated—see the warning on p. 67 for more information. Use sticks as tongs to lift the hot stones into your water. If you put several sizzling-hot stones in there, the water will boil. You can also boil water in a metal cup by setting it directly on hot coals. Heat until it reaches a full, bubbling boil, and keep it boiling for one minute. Then let the water sit until it is cool enough to drink.

If you have muddy water, you can first filter out the dirt with a bandanna or other piece of clothing. You can also pour the water through sand to get some of the mud out of it. If you have a fire, keep in mind that crushed charcoal from burned wood is great for both filtering water and making it taste better. Some people carry coffee filters when they hike, just in case they find muddy water. The coffee filters can also be used to start fires, and they don't weigh much, so they're easy to carry in your pack.

Don't forget that after you filter muddy water, you still have to boil or otherwise purify it.

Another way to get cleaner water from a muddy source is to dig a hole two or three feet away from the water. Water that's underground should seep into your hole, and after it sits for a while, it should clear. You can then take the cleaner water out of the hole and purify it.

SOLAR STILLS

If you can't find water, you can make a simple device to get some out of plants, grasses, mud, or even your own pee. This device is called a *solar still*.

I always have plastic bags and twist ties in my pack. One of the easiest ways to make a solar still is to simply tie a small clear plastic bag around the leaves of some nonpoisonous plant, such as willow or grass, that the sun is shining on. (See chapter 9, p. 138, for information on plants to avoid.) Tie it tightly so that it won't fall off when it becomes weighted down with water. Let the bag sit in the sun long enough to collect water from the leaves, but don't leave it too long. After it sits in the sun for hours, the water tastes really bad. Each bag can produce a good mouthful of water.

Another kind of solar still uses a gallon-size plastic food storage bag. Put a small, clean rock in one corner of the bag, then add enough grass, clover, or fresh leaves so that the bag is about three-fourths full. Only use leaves that you know are not poisonous. Scoop air into the bag and seal it tight. Then put the bag on a sunny slope, with the heavier corner that contains the rock positioned so that it's lower than the rest of the bag. (That way, the water will collect at one end.) In a few hours you will have water in the bottom of the bag. Drain the water into your bottle or cup, replace the used grass or leaves with fresh ones, and start the process again.

If you happen to have a piece of clear plastic sheeting and a cup or can, you can make a still in the ground. In a sunny spot, dig a bowl-shaped hole about one to two feet deep and not as wide as your plastic sheet. Make a depression at the bottom of the hole to set the cup in. Once your

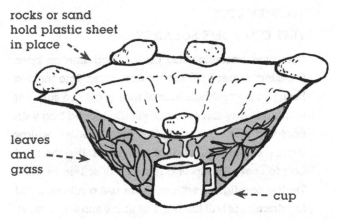

rocks or sand
hold plastic sheet
in place

leaves
and
grass

cup

cup is at the bottom, pack leaves or grass around the cup,
along the sides of your earth bowl. If you don't have any
leaves or grass, you can fill the bowl (not quite to the rim of
your cup) with dirty water, your own urine, sea water, pieces
of cactus, or damp earth. Drape the plastic sheet loosely
over the top of the bowl and anchor the edges with sand
or rocks. Set a small rock on top of the plastic so that it's
positioned just over the cup. When the moist substances
inside the bowl are heated by the sun, water will be drawn
out of them and collect on the plastic sheet. Since the rock
is the lowest point on the sheet, the water will run down
inside of the sheet and drip into your cup. I've found that
a ground still produces less water than any of the other
types of stills discussed here, and it definitely requires the
most work, but it's the only kind that can be used with substances other than leaves or grass.

ACTIVITY

TEST OUT SOME SOLAR STILLS

Use three sandwich-size plastic food storage bags to collect water from leaves and grass. Into the first bag, put several handfuls of torn grass (be sure not to include any dirt or roots). Fill the second bag with nontoxic plant materials like pine needles, willow leaves, or dandelions. Seal both bags. Use the third bag to cover the tip of a leafy bush or tree branch. Tie the bag tightly with string or use a rubber band to attach it. Let all the bags sit in the sun for an hour. Can you see the moisture that has collected in each bag? What type of plant gives the most water?

SIGNALING FOR HELP

Once you've created a shelter and made sure you have a supply of water, your main responsibility when lost in the wilderness will be signaling for help. You know that people are looking for you—in fact, you may have even heard people searching or seen a helicopter flying overhead. However, unless you've signaled for help, it's likely that no one has seen you. Why not? Think, for example, of a rescue helicopter flying over a forest. Imagine making a green dot on a piece of green paper. If you put the paper on the floor, stood over it, and looked for the green dot, would you be able to see it? Then imagine putting that paper on a floor that's carpeted with the same green paper. Would you be able to see the green dot? That is what the search area looks like to the helicopter pilot.

To attract the searchers' attention, you need to make yourself stand out more. There are many ways to do this, depending on where you are, what the weather is like, and the ways you think searchers might be looking for you.

WHISTLES AND AIR HORNS

Even if it's dark and no one can see you, they still might be able to hear you. Yelling for help is a good way to attract the attention of people who are fairly close to you. However, you can't yell for very long without getting hoarse or losing your voice, and the sound of a yell does not travel very far, especially in the deep woods or during a storm. A much better idea is to always carry a good whistle with you. Blowing a whistle doesn't take much more energy than breathing, and you won't lose your voice.

There are excellent plastic survival whistles that are twice as loud as regular whistles and can even be heard underwater. Some whistles contain a dried pea that causes the whistle to make sound—but, if the pea gets wet, the whistle won't work. Get one that is made without a pea inside, like a Storm whistle.

Many of my friends in search and rescue now carry small air horns with them in the wilderness. Not only are these loud horns good for signaling, but they also scare the heck out of bears and mountain lions. You can buy compact emergency horns that fit in your hand at outdoor or boating supply stores.

The universal signal for help is three loud noises, such as blasts of a whistle or air horn, with about a second of silence between each blast. (Be sure to cover your ears when you use a loud whistle or horn. These devices are so powerful that they can damage your hearing when you use them.) Do lots of three-blast sets, waiting a minute or so between each set. No whistle or horn? Hit a tree with a stick three times in a row, wait about a minute, and repeat.

FLASHLIGHTS AND CHEMICAL LIGHT STICKS

A flashlight (or headlamp) is also great for signaling after dark—you can help draw attention to the light by moving it back and forth. Be careful not to use up your batteries by keeping the light turned on all night.

Chemical light sticks, on the other hand, can be used only once but will light up your area for most of the night. However, someone has to be fairly close to you to see them. To use them, you just bend them until you hear a pop. Then shake them gently and they will give you light.

GROUND SIGNALS

To signal a helicopter or plane flying overhead, you first need to be in an open space, like a meadow. You have a better chance of being seen if you are wearing bright clothing in a color that stands out, like orange, or if you have an orange trash bag. Wave your trash bag or lie on your back in the clearing and move your arms and legs to make yourself appear larger and attract attention.

You could also make a sign on the ground. You *do not* have to spell out "HELP" or "SOS." Just make a big X on the ground with wood, rocks, or anything that can be seen from above. How about scraping snow away with your feet so that the earth underneath creates a dark X? Think *big*—the X has to be visible to a pilot flying far above. Make each one at least three times taller than your body.

Certain items in your survival kit (see chapter 12, p 191) can be used to create a ground signal:

- **Flagging tape.** Eight-foot-long strips of orange flagging tape, placed close together in rows in the shape of an X, can be seen from far above you. Make sure to hold the tape strips down with rocks or dirt so they don't blow away when your back is turned. You could also tie lots of long strips of flagging tape to a bush in an open space.

- **Flavored gelatin.** Since bright colors stand out especially well against a white snow background, one of the best things you can take with you in snow country is a box or two of cherry- or raspberry-flavored gelatin. Not only can you eat it for quick energy (it's full of sugar), but you can also scatter it over snow to make a big, easy-to-see X.

- **Mylar-lined tarp.** Often called *space blankets*, these pre-folded tarps are made of a silvery material that is great to use for signaling. You can fasten them to the ground or wave them to be seen.

SIGNAL MIRRORS AND SIGNAL FIRES

A signal mirror or signal fire can also be used to get the attention of helicopters or planes—and is useful for signaling distant rescuers on the ground, as well. A signal mirror is simply a mirror with a hole in the center. The hole allows you to look through the mirror in order to aim your signal. By tipping the mirror in your hand, you can direct a flash of sunlight at rescuers up to 50 miles away. If you signal to a plane or helicopter and it looks like the pilot has spotted you, please don't blind him or her with more flashes of light.

If you don't have a signal mirror but you do have a compass, it may have a mirror on it that you can use to signal for help. If you're near a car, you should be able to remove the rearview mirror pretty easily and use that. In fact, you can use anything that's really shiny, like a bright piece of metal or even a CD. To aim, hold the mirror in one hand and stretch the other hand out in front of you. Make a V shape with the fingers of your outstretched hand. Line up your target so that you can see it in the V, then direct the light flash toward the V by tilting the mirror in your other hand.

To make a signal fire, you need to clear a 10-foot-wide circle for safety—remove all flammable materials. Then start a hot fire in the center. (For instructions on how to build a fire, see chapter 5, p. 59.) When you see or hear searchers (in a plane, helicopter, boat, etc.) who might notice your signal, lay a small amount of wet leaves or fresh green materials over your burning fire. When you put moist or newly picked greens on a hot fire, large amounts of white smoke appear almost instantly. This takes some planning, since you will need to have your leaves or greens ready ahead of time. Make your fire big enough that it doesn't go out when you dump a load of wet leaves or fresh greens on top of it.

> **Do not use wet logs or branches—they can pop and send fiery sparks flying. And don't burn poison oak or poison ivy (see p. 143)—the smoke is dangerous.**

The best and safest spots to make a signal fire are sandy or rocky areas near water, away from anything that might catch fire. Avoid places with dried grass, pine needles, or hanging branches. More than one lost person has started a huge forest fire while trying to make a signal. Others have been seriously burned.

While smoke does make for a great signal, there's no getting around the fact that fires are dangerous. Mirrors are much safer and easier to signal with.

PAPER AND PEN

With a notepad and a waterproof pen, you can leave notes along your trail for rescuers to find. Write down what time it is and where you are going—for instance, if you are leaving the trail to get water or make a shelter—place the note in the middle of the trail, and use a rock to hold it down.

CELL PHONES AND WALKIE-TALKIES

A working cell phone is a terrific way to call for help, but there are still many areas of the country with no cell reception. If you cannot make calls, you may still be able to send a text message, so be sure to try that. These days, most cell phones have GPS (Global Positioning System) functions built into them. That means that even if you do not have a cell phone signal and you can't make a call, your cell phone company may be able to locate you. However, this only works if you have a GPS feature on your phone (your cell phone provider can tell you whether your phone has this feature), and you leave your cell phone turned on.

Many families now carry two-way family radio service devices, or walkie-talkies. These are great for staying in touch with others while on a hike. If you are carrying one when you get lost, try to find someone who's listening on the other end. Talk on each channel and listen for a response.

BUILDING A FIRE

The ability to build a fire is a great skill to have. A campfire can make you feel safe and keep you warm. It can scare away wild animals and serve as a signal to searchers in the night. In some cases, it can save your life. But it can also make your situation much worse—you can burn yourself, set your shelter on fire, or burn down the forest.

A fire needs air, heat, and fuel to burn. It sounds simple, but if you have ever tried to start a campfire on a rainy day, you know how difficult it can be. If you are tired and scared and it's dark outside, it becomes even harder. You could use an entire book of matches and never get a fire going. Then what would you do?

PREPARING YOUR FIRE AREA

To make things easier, pick a spot that is already fire safe, like the top of a large rock or a sandy area. Your fire needs to be out of the wind; if possible, it should have a boulder or a rock wall behind it. If you build a fire next to a large rock, more of the heat reflects back to you, keeping you warmer.

To be smart and safe, clear a circle at least 10 feet wide for your fire area. Remove flammable leaves, grasses, and pine needles. If possible, dig a hole in the ground a few inches deep to make a fire pit. This makes your fire not only safer but also easier to light if there is a breeze. If you can't dig a pit, a ring of rocks placed around your fire will help to contain the flames, and the rocks will stay heated for a while after the fire burns down. If you're lost in a snowy area, you can't start a fire on top of snow itself, of course. You must build it on a deck of logs or large sticks.

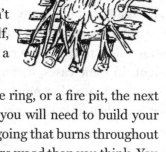

After you make a deck, a fire ring, or a fire pit, the next step is to gather the materials you will need to build your fire. In order to get a good fire going that burns throughout the night, you will need way more wood than you think. You will need tiny pieces of tinder, small kindling sticks, and logs. *Tinder* is what you light first, and *kindling* are thin sticks and branches that feed the fire to get it going. Tinder needs to be *completely dry*, and the fluffier the better.

TINDER TYPES

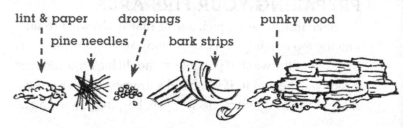

lint & paper   droppings   punky wood

pine needles   bark strips

You can save time and effort by carrying tinder in your survival kit. Good tinder materials include fine steel wool, shredded paper, waxed paper, or small pieces of fatwood (a type of resinous tree). You can also check your pockets for dryer lint; it is usually dry and makes a good tinder.

If you didn't bring tinder and the weather is wet, look for dry pine needles or grass, dried rabbit or deer droppings, and small pieces of wood or bark. If you can't find dry tinder on the ground, your best bet is to use *punk*, which is rotted wood found inside trees that have been dead for some time. Bark from birch or cedar trees can also be shredded and used as tinder to start a fire. Birch trees have white, papery bark, and cedar trees look like redwood trees or pines but have flat leaves. Break it up or shred it so it forms a loose bundle.

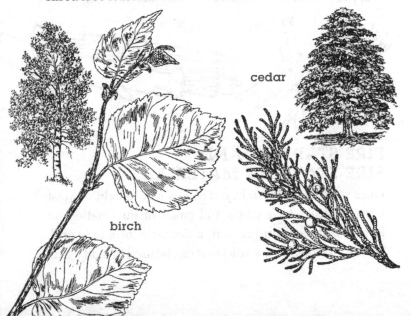

cedar

birch

Search for firewood in places that are protected from the weather—perhaps under a big tree or beneath a piece of bark. Once you have a fire going, you can place damp wood next to your fire to dry so you can use it later.

There are many good ways to build a fire, but you'll always start by lighting small pieces of dry tinder. The tinder must be arranged so that the flames are protected from the wind but still can get a little oxygen. You can either make a tepee of tinder and small sticks or you can lean a tinder bundle against a log. Once you see flames in your tinder, blow on the fire gently to add oxygen and carefully feed it with small kindling sticks. Only add a stick or two at a time until the fire is burning well. After you have a strong fire, you can start adding larger sticks, and later, logs.

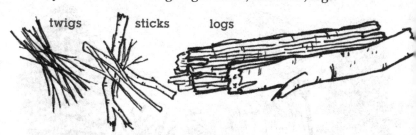

twigs   sticks   logs

FIRE STARTERS AND FIRE-STARTING MATERIALS

Once your tinder is ready, you need a way to light it. Most survival books have pages and pages of information on how to start a fire using flint, a fire plow, or a bow drill. With flint, you create sparks that can be used to light a fire;

with fire plows and bow drills, you rub two sticks together to create friction and heat. While it is fun to learn these methods, they are not very practical ways to start a fire. If you are cold, scared, wet, and all alone in the woods, you need a way to start a fire that's quick, easy, and foolproof.

Camping stores sell wonderful products that help you to get a fire started. Waterproof matches light easily, even in wet weather, but they need dry striker paper. Pack them in a sealed container to keep the striker dry. Disposable lighters are cheap, and they usually work even if they have gotten wet; you just need to dry them out. You should carry both waterproof matches and a lighter whenever you go hiking.

If it's sunny, you can use a small magnifying glass or even a pair of eyeglasses to start a fire. In fact, anything that reflects sunlight can create a fire. Fires have been ignited as a result of glass bowls on wood decks, crystals hanging in windows, and even drinking glasses left on windowsills.

ACTIVITY Can you make a fire with a small magnifying glass? Hold it steady and aim it at a bunch of dry tinder. Be patient—it will take a few minutes to light your fire. How about an empty soda can and a piece of chocolate? Rub the chocolate on the bottom of the can, first with your fingers and then with a rag. After a lot of rubbing, the metal will become shiny and reflective, and the curved surface of the can bottom concentrates the sunlight into a small beam that creates heat. Tip the can to reflect sunlight onto dry tinder until it smokes and catches fire.

In addition to matches and a lighter, you should also bring fire-starting materials—substances that you can place amid your tinder and light quickly in order to get the fire going. Some fire-starting materials can be purchased; others can be made at home:

- **Tortilla chips.** If you hold the flame from a match or a lighter under a tortilla chip such as a Dorito for a few seconds, it will catch fire. Light-colored chips that don't have much seasoning on them are easiest to light (seasoning seems to make them less flammable). Corn chips work well too, as do plain old potato chips.

- **Toilet paper and candle wax.** Coat individual toilet paper squares with melted candle wax. These will catch fire immediately, and they'll burn steadily for quite a while. Dryer lint coated with melted candle wax also makes good fire-starting material.

- **Cotton balls and petroleum jelly.** Dip cotton balls in petroleum jelly (Vaseline). These, too, will catch fire immediately, and they'll burn strongly with a big flame, long enough to light your tinder.

- **Fire paste.** Sold in tubes, it is squeezed directly onto wood and then lit. It ignites immediately.

- **Fuel tablets.** There are many different types of solid

fuel tablets that burn well and provide enough
sustained heat to cook over.

- **Magnesium block scrapings.** Magnesium is sold
  in blocks that have a flint edge on one side for
  creating sparks. Using a knife, you shave a small pile
  of the magnesium flakes onto your tinder. Then you
  strike the flint with your knife to create a spark that
  lights the magnesium flakes on fire (or you can just
  use a match or a lighter to light them). Magnesium
  catches fire even when it's damp.

If you didn't bring fire-starting materials, think about
the materials you did bring that could be used as a substitute. Is there lint in your pocket? Do you have tissues? A
candy bar wrapper? A corner of a map you can tear off and
shred?

I usually carry a magnesium block (as well as a lighter
and a candle) with me when I'm exploring the wilderness.
The back of a knife blade or the saw blade of a Swiss Army
knife or other multi-tool works best for shaving flakes off
the magnesium block (be careful to cut away from you).
The saw blade's rough surfaces are also great for creating
sparks by striking it against your flint strip. Scrape the
blade up the flint edge of your magnesium block and aim
the sparks to your shavings. This is an effective way to start
a fire, but it does take a lot practice to become good at it.
You can also use a fire steel, which is a little rod that has an
attached piece of toothed steel. The steel is used to create a
shower of hot sparks by scraping it quickly over the rod.

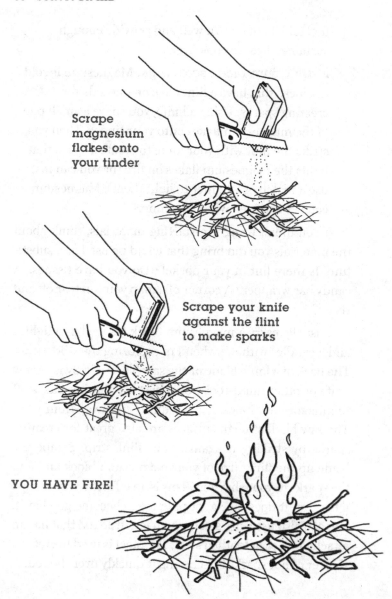

Scrape magnesium flakes onto your tinder

Scrape your knife against the flint to make sparks

YOU HAVE FIRE!

ACTIVITY With adult supervision, practice making a fire in a small pit using a knife, magnesium, and a flint strip. It does take practice to learn how to make this work.

KEEPING WARM AND KEEPING SAFE

To stay warm at night, heat some rocks next to the fire to put under your clothes or in your shelter. Remember that they are hot, so don't burn yourself. They may need an hour or so to cool down before you handle them. Even then, you may need to use your socks over your hands to carry them.

☒ Do not put a rock next to or into the fire if the rock has been sitting in water or has small pockets or cracks that could trap water. (For example, lava rocks are full of small holes that might hold water.) Any little pockets of water inside a rock can cause the rock to suddenly explode when it's heated.

Always be careful when picking up any rock. I found plenty of rattlesnakes and scorpions hiding under rocks when I was young. I quickly learned to use a stick to flip over rocks before reaching down to pick them up with my hands.

If you are stranded for more than one day, or you just have extra time on your hands, you can build a large fire in a trench the size of your body. After the fire burns down to coals, cover the entire fire bed with a few inches of sand or dirt. Place some green branches on top of the sand or dirt, and you will have a nice warm bed to sleep on. (The branches will help to prevent you from accidentally uncovering the coals while you sleep.) Another way to create a heated bed is to build a fire on a large rock that you plan to sleep on. After you brush off the coals, the rock will be hot for many hours.

Whenever you leave your camp, *always extinguish the fire*. If possible, pour water on the fire and stir it with a stick to make sure it is out. If you have no water, cover the fire with a thick layer of dirt or sand. Be sure the fire is completely out before you take off. Many forest fires and brush fires have started from campfires that were supposed to be out, but instead smoldered for hours until the dirt that covered them was blown away and hot embers flew out.

AVOIDING DANGEROUS ANIMALS

I showed up for search and rescue training one icy morning, recovering from pneumonia. I was too sick to work my dog, so I volunteered to be a subject for all the other search dogs. Armed with blankets, two types of camouflage, and a sleeping pad, I covered myself completely and curled up on the frozen ground. I was so comfortable and warm that I fell asleep, and I only woke when I heard one of the search dogs circling me about six feet away. I waited for a cold nose to pop under the layers of blankets and camouflage, but the dog walked around me twice and left.

Eventually, all the dogs found me, and I packed up my blankets and headed back to base. Twenty feet from my temporary bed, I discovered the paw print of a mountain lion. It was so fresh that I could see the texture of the toes in the recently thawed mud. Only then did I realize that it was a lion, not a search dog, that had circled around me, probably sniffing the mound of human-smelling blankets and tarps. That was not my first or last mountain lion encounter, but it remains my most memorable. It still makes me laugh, but I have a weird sense of humor.

DON'T BE SCARED—BE PREPARED!

If you're like most kids, the scariest thing about being lost at night is the thought that you share the wilderness with large, hungry predators, venomous snakes, or other dangerous animals. What are your chances of being attacked? Is it safe to go to sleep in your shelter? What should you do if you see a bear or a cougar? How safe are you?

Relax. Although humans are occasionally attacked by wild animals, it's rare. For instance, many people are terrified of mountain lions—after all, there are thousands of mountain lions out in the woods, meadows, and even suburban neighborhoods—but people don't realize that in the past 120 years, only 20 people in the entire United States have been killed by one. That's an average of just one fatal attack every *six years!*

The animals you are most likely to hear outside your shelter at night are not dangerous. That rustling sound is probably being made by a deer, raccoon, or mouse. Even if the sound is coming from something more dangerous, you need to take a deep breath and remember this: thousands of people see dangerous animals every year but don't get attacked by them.

If you hike frequently, you probably pass by several dangerous animals on a regular basis without knowing it. I walk my dogs in the forest all the time, and we pass piles of mountain lion scat every day. Just about everyone I know hikes, camps, fishes, and hunts, and we have all had experiences with venomous snakes and other wild animals. *Not one person I know* has ever been hurt by an animal while enjoying these activities. Why? Because we don't do things that will put us in danger. We know what to do when we come across a wild animal and we are prepared for emergencies.

Now you can be prepared, too. There is a famous saying: "Knowledge is power." If you know what animals are out there, which ones might be dangerous, and what to do if you encounter them, you gain power, so that you can go out and enjoy yourself in the wilderness without fear.

Later sections in this chapter will show what to do if you encounter a particular animal—a mountain lion, a bear, a venomous snake, etc. But first, here are some basic rules for dealing with *any* animal you may encounter in the wilderness:

- **Leave wild animals alone**. The most important rule to remember is to give wild animals space. Most animals, even the dangerous ones, just want to get away from you. Give them a way out. An amazing number of people think it's OK to crowd a wild animal to take a picture of it or get a closer look. Animals don't like strangers sticking cameras in their faces any more than you would. Do not corner *any* wild animal unless you are prepared for a fight. Many people have been surprised to find themselves bitten by cute little squirrels or chased by deer. Even if an animal seems totally harmless, you should still stay away. Some small animals carry diseases that can spread to humans; others, such as certain tiny toads and salamanders, have poisons on their skin that are toxic to both humans and dogs.

- **Don't hike alone.** Wild animals don't attack groups of people. One of the safest things you can do is hike with several other people. The more, the better. And stay together. Your chances of being bothered by any large animal is next to nothing if you are in a group. If you can't hike with a group of people, at least go with a buddy.

- **Bring some protection.** If you hike with your family in bear country, talk to your parents about carrying bear spray on your hikes. Bear spray is made from hot peppers and is specially formulated to scare off dangerous large animals. Remember—*any type of pepper spray is a weapon, not a toy*, and it is a crime to use it on people. In addition, be aware that in many states, it's illegal for a person younger than 18 years old to carry pepper spray. Find out what the law is in your state and talk to your parents about it. If you can't carry pepper spray, there are other options. I sometimes carry a large walking stick with me when hiking. Animals such coyotes, bears, and mountain lions are generally fearful when you carry something that looks like a weapon. Sticks are free, legal, and easy to find. They are also good for checking for snakes in tall grass and helping you walk over rough ground. You could also carry a small but extremely loud air horn. The noise scares bears and mountain lions away. No matter what form of protection you decide to carry, do not bury it in your pack where you can't reach it easily. Keep it on your belt or in your hand.

- **Use your animal instinct.** Whenever I've been watched or followed by a mountain lion, even if I never saw it, its presence made me uncomfortable. Other people have reported experiencing the same kind of creepy feeling long before they realized that a lion was around. Pay attention to your feelings. And if you are hiking with dogs, watch their behavior. Once when I was hiking near Lake Tahoe in California, I was followed for over a mile by a mountain lion. I never got a glimpse of it, but my two German shepherds were jumpy and kept looking around the whole time. On our return trip, I found the lion's tracks covering the dogs' and my footprints. It had been right behind us, following our trail.

- **Look around.** When you hike, don't just look ahead or to the right and left. Check all around you for signs of wild animals—look behind you; look up at ledges and rock piles; look in trees. If you know what to look for, animal signs will tell you a story. Know some basic animal tracks and be alert if you find fresh signs of predators. When there are bears nearby, you will see their footprints and large piles of bear scat. Their droppings often have berries in them. You might also find old logs that have been torn apart, claw marks on trees, or bits of bear fur on bark. Male cougars leave *scrapes*, which are small piles of leaves and debris with urine on them, to mark their territory. Cougars also scratch tree trunks and leave scat next to trails. Their scat usually contains deer hair and bits of bone. You might also find a deer carcass or a pile of animal bones. Both cougars and bears stay close to their kills for several days, so if you find a freshly killed animal, get out of there. Foxes like to poop on top of logs or rocks, and coyotes like to poop at trail intersections. See the resources section (p. 207) for websites and books that can teach you more about animal tracks and scat.

ANIMAL SCAT

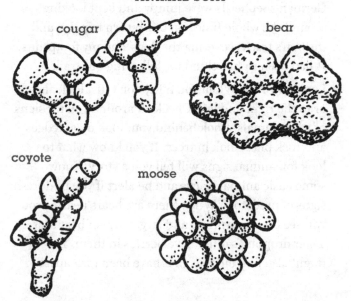

cougar

bear

coyote

moose

ACTIVITY
CASTING ANIMAL TRACKS

Taking plaster casts of animal tracks is not only fun but also a good way to practice finding and identifying footprints in the wilderness. You can start a track collection of your own.

What you need:

- Scissors
- Ruler
- 32-ounce plastic soda bottle, empty and clean
- 1 box of plaster of Paris (available at hardware and crafts stores)
- 1 quart- or gallon-size plastic food storage bag
- 8- to 16-ounce bottle of water

Search an outdoor area until you find a good animal print to cast. Casts work best in soft but not squishy mud. Using your scissors and ruler, cut a 2-inch-wide ring out of the center of the soda bottle to use for the outer border of your cast. Bring the plaster of Paris, bag, bottle of water, and soda bottle ring to your footprint.

Set the ring around your chosen track, pressing it into the ground so it makes a sturdy wall around your print. Next, pour about a cup (about 8 ounces) of water into your bag and add plaster of Paris according to the mixing directions on the box. Gently mix together the water and plaster of Paris by squeezing the bag until you have a thick batter. Mix gently and thoroughly so you don't create air bubbles. Holding the top of the bag closed, gently tap the bag against the ground to get rid of any bubbles that were created. Then, slowly pour your plaster onto the ground inside your ring—but not directly onto the animal track. Let the plaster seep into the track from the sides so you don't ruin it.

Let the plaster sit for at least an hour to harden. (The plaster will become solid in half that time, but it takes longer for it to become sturdy enough to handle.) Remove your plaster cast from the ground by digging gently around the edges and carefully lifting it up. Drying plaster feels warm. When it is cool, you can carefully clean it with a cloth or soft brush.

MOUNTAIN LIONS

One warm Saturday in the town of Cool, California, I was walking my dog on a popular paved trail that is frequently used by bicyclists, people on horseback, and runners. All around me were families with kids, fellow dog walkers, and joggers. Suddenly, in a meadow next to the road, I spotted what looked like the head of a large mountain lion poking out of the grass. I stared at the head, then laughed to myself. "Oh, it's just an oak stump," I thought. Then the stump twitched an ear. It *was* a mountain lion! I held my

MOUNTAIN LION

dog's collar firmly and said loudly, "Hey there, big kitty." The huge cat jumped up and bounded into the nearby brush. All those other people on the road with me had passed right by this big lion without noticing him, and he had been content to sit in the sun and watch the parade of dogs, horses, and people go by.

Mountain lions are known by many names, including puma, cougar, wildcat, panther, and catamount. These impressive large cats weigh hundreds of pounds and can leap 20 feet in one jump. They typically feed on deer. In the United States, mountain lions commonly live along the West Coast, in the Great Plains, and in the Southwest. They are also commonly found in Mexico and in the southwestern area of Canada. There are also small populations in Florida, and they have been spotted in other states as well. If you live in the Midwest or the eastern United States, you probably do not have to worry about mountain lions. In fact, no matter where you live, it is possible that you will never see a single mountain lion. Although there are at least 50,000 of them in the United States, they usually try to hide from people. They are most active from just before dark to the early morning.

When you pull a string on the floor in front of your cat at home, it will pounce on it. In the same way, mountain lions often follow anything that's moving quickly, including runners, bike riders, and animals. Mountain lions are especially drawn to anything that suddenly breaks into a run (which is what many people do when confronted with a lion), to dogs (particularly small ones), and to little kids who are running around.

When you are hiking in an area of the country where mountain lions live, look behind you frequently as you walk. Don't forget to look up at ledges, trees, and hills, as well. If you find a fresh kill, like a dead deer, get out of the area. Mountain lions usually stay close to their kills. Hike in a group and don't let younger children get out of your sight. Keep your dog close to you.

If you see a mountain lion, *do not* turn your back on it. Never crouch down or bend over. And *never try to run away from it*. When you are faced with a dangerous wild animal, the most important thing to remember is not to run, scream, or panic. You will only make things worse. The following chart shows the actions the experts say you should take when you encounter a mountain lion.

LION'S ACTIONS	DANGER LEVEL	WHAT YOU SHOULD DO
Lion is far away—not paying attention to you.	*Low*	Stay in groups. Don't run around or talk excitedly. Keep your eyes on the lion, and don't block its exit.
Lion is following you, watching you, but is more than 50 yards away.*	*Medium* (Adults) *High* (Kids)	Lion is curious. *Do not* turn your back, run, bend over, or kneel down. Try and grab weapons like sticks or rocks without bending over. Kids should stand together in a group, or behind adults. Stand up straight and look as big as possible. If you can back away slowly, do it.
Lion is staring at you and is less than 50 yards away.*	*High*	Lion is wondering if it should attack. If you can get into a car or safe location without turning your back, do it. *Do not run.* Look big. Raise your jacket over your head, shout in a deep loud voice, and keep in a group.
Lion is crouching or crawling toward you; its tail is twitching and it is staring at you very intently.	*Very High*	Lion is about to attack and is looking for a way to do it. If you have rocks, throw them. Get your pepper spray out if you have it. Show your teeth and growl. Make scary faces, and move slowly to put a rock or tree between you and the lion, but *do not take your eyes off the lion.* Don't move to lower ground.
Lion's ears are flattened; its rear legs may be moving up and down or pumping.	*Attack*	You are about to be attacked. Get ready to defend yourself. Some attacks can be stopped by rushing toward the lion with a large stick raised up like a weapon. Use pepper spray. If the lion is right next to you, poke it in the eyes and mouth with your stick, but stay away from its paws and teeth.

* 50 yards is half the length of a football field

BEARS

When I was young, my Girl Scout troop went camping in Yosemite National Park in California. We slept in a mass of sleeping bags on the open ground. I woke in the middle of the night to find a large black bear standing two feet from my head, sniffing at the pillow of the girl next to me. Before I dove to the bottom of my sleeping bag in terror, I saw the bear roll the girl over to get to the candy bars she had stuffed under her pillow. She slept through the whole thing, but it took me years to overcome my fear of bears.

BLACK
BEAR

Nowadays people are a lot smarter about bears. They know not to leave food around their campsites that might tempt the animals to visit. Hikers know that they need to hang their food high up in a tree at night and avoid wearing lotions that smell like food. Since that first encounter, I have met many more black bears, both in the woods and in my own yard. I give them the respect that they deserve and stay away, and I have never had a bad experience with any of them.

In some northern states, especially the northwestern states, there are grizzly bears, also known as brown bears, as well as black bears. In the United States, grizzly bears are responsible for more attacks than black bears.

It is estimated that about 750,000 black bears live in the United States and Canada. They live in mountainous or swampy areas throughout the United States, but they are seldom found in the Southwest, Great Plains, or Midwest regions. Grizzly bears are less common; there are fewer than 2,000 in the continental United States, about 30,000 in Alaska, and approximately 20,000 in Canada. They are found in Canada, Alaska, Washington State, Montana, Wyoming, and Idaho.

The most common reason that bears attack people is because they become startled when they suddenly encounter a human. When you are hiking in bear country, *make noise* to warn bears that you are in the area. *Bear bells*

GRIZZLY BEAR

help—these are little bells worn by both people and dogs. Even better, you can clap your hands and yell every few minutes. Do not run along trails where you might surprise a bear. Be extra careful near noisy rivers or creeks, where bears might not hear you, or near food sources such as blackberry patches, salmon spawning grounds, or a freshly killed animal carcass.

Bears have also been known to attack because they are hungry or because a mother bear senses that her young are in danger. Staying safe in bear country depends on avoiding bears or reassuring them that you are not a threat to them or their cubs.

If you see a bear, leave the area. Bears may attack without warning. Or they may show that they are upset by swaying their heads, making huffing noises, and clacking their teeth. If they pin their ears back, they are showing that they are tense. When they stand on their hind legs, they may be trying to get a better view of you.

Keep your dog near you. Although dogs often "tree" bears—chase them up a tree—they have also been known to lead unwanted bears back to their owners: a bear spots a dog that is running through the woods, becomes upset or curious, and follows it right back to you.

Bears are also attracted to the smell of food. When you're in bear country, try to cook at a site at least 50 yards—half the length of a football field—from your shelter, and do not keep food items of any kind in your camp. If possible, don't even keep clothes that smell like food in camp. A bear's sense of smell is a thousand times better than ours, so burying food or putting clothing in a bag will not help much. Also, don't use a fruity-smelling lip balm, sunscreen, lotion, shampoo, soap, or perfume. You don't want to make yourself smell yummy to a bear.

To help keep yourself and your food safe, hang it (as well as your lip balm, sunscreen, and any other item that has a scent) from a tree at least 50 yards from your shelter. Put the food and other items in a sturdy bag or wrap everything in clothing, then tie a rope to the bag or bundle using a secure knot like a bowline. (See chapter 2, p. 20, for knot-tying instructions.) You will need to hang the items at least 12 feet off the ground and 10 feet away from the tree. (Remember, 10 feet is the same height as a basketball hoop.) You can tie a rock to the free end of the rope and throw the rock over the tree limb from which you are going to hang your bundle. Pull your bag up into the air, then tie the free end of the rope to the tree trunk, using a clove hitch knot so you can adjust the length of your rope. This will usually protect your supplies from both bears and the forest's biggest thieves—raccoons. I have been told that raccoons can untie knots and gnaw through rope, so do your best to make your food difficult to reach. I have seen raccoons open doorknobs and unlatch cupboards, so I am sure that knots are not a big problem to them. They have clever little hands.

Some areas in bear country now require that you carry and store all food, garbage, and scented items in a *bear canister*. Bear canisters are hard-sided containers that hold all these items and should be placed 100 feet away from your shelter, on flat ground. You do not want to leave the canister on a hill, because it could get knocked over and roll down the hill. Bear canisters can be carried in your pack and have been proven to keep your food safe from both bears and raccoons.

BEAR'S ACTIONS	WHAT YOU SHOULD DO
Bear is far away, not paying attention to you.	Turn around and slowly backtrack your steps along the trail. Keep walking for 15 minutes. Then take another trail. If you have to go back up the trail where you saw the bear, wait 15–20 minutes before you head out.
Bear is nearby or on your trail, but not close enough to become alarmed by you.	Keeping your eyes on the bear, back away from it. Get out your bear spray, if you have some, and keep moving slowly away from the bear. *Do not* make eye contact with it. Back away about 400 yards.*
Bear is at close range.	Don't panic. Don't run. Don't scream. Any of those actions can make a bear attack. Talk soothingly to the bear, but don't make eye contact with it and do not bend over. Back away if the bear is not acting aggressively. Stop moving if it looks like your activity is upsetting the bear.
Bear charges you.	Even now, *don't panic*. Most charges are bluffs. If the bear doesn't stop, spray him in the face with pepper spray. If you don't have spray, drop a hat or another item (not your pack and not food) and back away quickly. The bear may be distracted and stop to examine the item.
Bear attacks you.	Most bear attacks are defensive attacks, and once the bear decides that you are not a threat, it will just leave. Curl up into a ball to protect your vital areas, cover your head and neck with your arms, and play dead. If you are wearing a pack, lie on your stomach with your pack protecting your back. Do not move until you are sure the bear is gone.

* 400 yards is the length of four football fields

In a survival situation, you may not be able to cook far away from your shelter, but do try to hang or store your food some distance away, and bury your garbage as far from your shelter as possible.

HOW GOING TO THE BATHROOM CAN ATTRACT BEARS AND MOUNTAIN LIONS

It's always a good idea to bring toilet paper and hand sanitizer with you whenever you explore the outdoors. If necessary, you can use leaves or grass in place of toilet paper; just be sure not to use anything that will cause a rash, like poison oak (see p. 143). That sounds obvious, but people still forget and grab whatever plant is handy.

Most experts say that human feces and urine will draw bears and mountain lions to you and your camp. Smaller animals are also attracted to urine because of the salts and minerals in it. And smaller animals often bring big animals back to you. When you're in the woods, think like a cat: dig a hole and go to the bathroom in it, then cover it completely when you are finished. If you can pee into a river or a large lake, instead of on land, that's even better. Moving water will carry your scent away from you. But please do not *ever* contaminate water by pooping in it.

You should go to the bathroom at least 100 yards away from your camp (again, that's the length of a football field). Pick a direction where the wind will not blow any scent toward your camp. By taking these steps, you not only keep the area clean, but you also might just keep the big predator animals away from your camp.

If it's the middle of the night and you don't have a flashlight, it can be dangerous to walk a hundred yards through the wilderness in the dark. In that case, you would be better off digging a hole near your shelter and burying your pee.

PIGS AND JAVELINAS

Feral, or wild, pigs are common in many parts of the country. It's estimated that there are four million feral pigs in the United States, and each one can weigh hundreds of pounds. However, only a handful of attacks on humans have been recorded. Wild pigs are found in small numbers in many states, but they are most common along the West Coast and in southern and southwestern states. Because they cause so much crop damage and reproduce rapidly, the US government considers them pests. Unless they're cornered, injured, or guarding young, feral pigs will run from humans. For this reason, they are not considered dangerous.

FERAL PIG

JAVELINA

However, another animal—one commonly mistaken for a feral pig—is especially aggressive and should be avoided. Javelinas, or collared peccaries, are piglike animals that live in the desert areas of the United States. Unlike feral pigs, javelinas are slender and small, and they usually weigh less than 50 pounds. The javelina has a gray-and-black coat with a white ring around the neck. Javelinas have been known to attack humans and dogs for no apparent reason. If you see one, quickly go another direction. If you are confronted by one, make noise, throw rocks, and use pepper spray if you have it. If your dog is attacked, run away and try to get your dog to come with you.

MOOSE

A moose can weigh over a thousand pounds, and its tracks look like deer or elk tracks but are about as long as an adult's hand—which is twice as large as an elk's and almost three times the size of a deer's. Moose live in the Rocky Mountains in Colorado and in the far northern areas of the

United States, and there are small populations in Washington State, Montana, Wyoming, Idaho, Utah, Maine, Minnesota, Michigan, New York, Vermont, and New Hampshire. They are most common, however, in Canada and Alaska.

In Alaska, more people are attacked by moose than by bears. Moose are aggressive in the fall mating season, and they will chase humans if they feel trapped, are especially hungry, or feel threatened by their dogs. If a moose licks its lips and puts its head down and the hair on its neck and back sticks up, back away. Always make sure the moose has an escape route. You might also look for a tree to climb or something to hide behind.

Sometimes, just like bears, moose make false charges in an attempt to scare you away. Actual attacks on humans by moose are very rare. As long as you remember not to block a moose's exit or get too close to it, you should be fine.

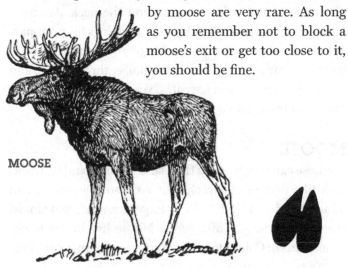

MOOSE

WOLVES

In practically every old cowboy movie I ever saw as a kid, somebody ended up getting attacked by a wolf. I know people who are terrified to go into the woods for fear of wolves, even though they live in states where wolves haven't been seen in more than a hundred years. Most wolves live in Canada and Alaska, but they also can be found in Arizona, New Mexico, Michigan, Minnesota, Wisconsin, Idaho, Washington State, Wyoming, and Montana. Fewer than 30 humans have been attacked by wolves in the United States and Canada in the past 200 years.

These beautiful animals are generally shy and avoid humans. If you're in wolf country, let wolves know you are in the area by clapping your hands and making other kinds of noise, just like you would in bear country. Wolves attack dogs much more often than they do humans, so keep your dog close or it could be attacked. Most kids will never see a wild wolf, but if you do, make yourself appear as big and tall as you can, throw things, yell, and back away. Do not make eye contact with the wolf. If it continues to approach you, keep yelling, throwing things, and making yourself look bigger to show it that you are too dangerous to attack.

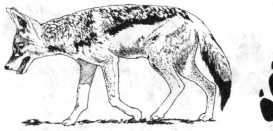

COYOTES

Anyone who has spent any time in the wild has probably seen a coyote. In fact, coyotes can also be found in big cities and suburbs almost everywhere in the United States. They come in all sizes and can be as small as a cocker spaniel or as big as a German shepherd. Long ago, coyotes in some areas mated with wolves, and their descendants are now much larger than other coyotes.

Coyotes are, for the most part, shy and afraid of people, and you usually can scare one away by throwing sticks, yelling, and making other loud noises. There have been fewer than 30 coyote attacks on humans in the United States since the 1800s, and most of the victims were not badly hurt. Most attacks on humans have taken place in areas where coyotes got used to living close to people and getting food from them, either because people fed them directly or because the coyotes were able to eat people's garbage or food left out for pets. If you live in a coyote-inhabited area, you should never feed your pets outside or make it easy for coyotes or other wild animals to get into and eat garbage, bird seed, or other attractive items.

Although coyote attacks on humans are rare, coyotes are more likely to attack small children than bigger kids or adults. In addition, coyotes consider dogs and cats to be food. A coyote may try to lure your dog away from you to "play." Once it does, the coyote and its pack will trap and attack the dog. My best advice to you is to keep your dog near you and on a leash anytime you are outside where coyotes or other dangerous wild animals may be present.

VENOMOUS SNAKES

Every year, hundreds of harmless snakes are killed by people who can't tell a venomous snake from a nonvenomous one. In the United States, there are only four species of snakes that are of any real danger to you:

- **Rattlesnakes.** In most states, these are the only venomous snakes you need to worry about. Rattlesnakes can be found almost anywhere. Once while treading water in a pond, I saw one swimming just a few feet from my face. I have found rattlesnakes in streams, in the desert, in city suburbs, and on woodland trails. There are many different kinds of rattlesnakes; they range in length from a few inches to over six feet, and they come in hundreds of different colors and patterns. I have seen

pink and orange ones that blended with the red earth in the Southwest and pure black ones that matched their lava rock homes in New Mexico. All rattlesnakes have triangular heads and thick bodies, but the best way to recognize them is by the rattle on their tails. Look for the rattle itself instead of listening for it or watching the snake's behavior—rattlesnakes do not always rattle, while harmless gopher snakes and bull snakes often shake their tails and coil their bodies to make you think they're rattlesnakes so that you'll leave them alone.

- **Copperheads.** These colorful snakes are found in

southern and eastern states in both swampy areas and forests, especially around rock piles and old buildings. They are almost invisible when they're coiled up among the leaves, and they often "freeze" when people are near. Like rattlesnakes, they have thick bodies and triangular heads. Copperheads are generally tan, orange, or pink, and most have light-colored blotches or bands bordered by a dark color in a pattern down their backs.

- **Water moccasins (cottonmouths).** There is only one kind of venomous water snake in the United States, and that is the water moccasin. This snake is also called a cottonmouth because when it's

threatened, it opens its
mouth very wide and tips
its head back to show the
white inside its mouth and
its fangs. Water moccasins
are found in or near water

throughout Texas, Alabama, Louisiana, Florida,
Georgia, Mississippi, Arkansas, Missouri, South
Carolina, North Carolina, Tennessee, and Kentucky
and in small areas of Illinois and Indiana. They
have large, heavy bodies and big triangular heads.
Water moccasins are sometimes hard to identify
because they come in different colors and patterns.
They can be dark brown, light brown, greenish
brown, or black. Young ones are often brightly
colored, with blotches of color in uneven bands
across their body. The youngsters look very much
like copperheads. Many have faint stripes around
their bodies. Many people claim that water moccasins
are aggressive. It is true that oftentimes a water
moccasin will "stand its ground" instead of slithering
away when you approach—but it's your job to avoid
them and move away from them.

- **Coral snakes**. Coral snakes, which are related to
  cobras, live in the southern part of the United States.
  Because they have to actually chew on a victim to
  inject their venom, their bites are often less
  dangerous than those of rattlesnakes, copperheads or

water moccasins. The coral snake has a slim body ringed with yellow, red, and black bands, and it is the only venomous snake in the United States that has round eye pupils and a slender head. Several types of nonvenomous snakes look very much like coral snakes—both scarlet king snakes and milk snakes also have red, black, and yellow bands. However, coral snakes have red bands that are bordered on either side by yellow bands, while nonvenomous snakes have red bands that are bordered on either side by black bands. You can memorize a famous rhyme to help you figure out whether a snake that looks like a coral snake is actually something else: "Red on black is friend to Jack. Red on yellow will kill a fellow."

Rattlesnakes, water moccasins, and copperheads are all members of a subfamily of venomous snakes called *pit vipers*. The diagram on the top of the opposite page shows some of the common differences between pit vipers and all of the many nonvenomous snakes in the United States and Canada. Coral snakes, on the other hand, are not pit vipers, and they can easily be mistaken for similar-looking nonvenomous snakes. If you are in coral snake territory, watch for that distinctive pattern of bands, as illustrated in the diagram on the bottom of the opposite page.

VENOMOUS PIT VIPER	NONVENOMOUS SNAKE

- large, triangular head
- vertical pupils
- thick, heavy body

- slender head
- round pupils
- slim body

MILK SNAKE
"Red on black is friend to Jack"

CORAL SNAKE
"Red on yellow will kill a fellow"
(red bands bordered by yellow)

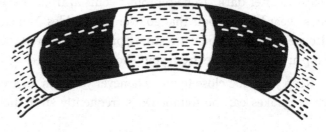

All snakes have one thing in common: they just want to be left alone. Most life-threatening snakebites can be prevented simply by being very careful to stay at least 10 feet away from any venomous snake. Keep in mind that a large snake can lift its head over a foot and a half off the ground and strike over a distance that equals about a third of its body length. No one should have to warn you not to mess with a rattlesnake! Yet each year, many people are bitten while bothering, trying to kill, or capturing a rattler.

In addition, many people are bitten each year when they disturb a snake accidentally. They may climb over logs or rocks without having a clear view of the other side, or they may put their hands someplace without first checking to see what's there. The most important thing you can do to keep from being bitten is to *watch your hands and feet*: step on top of logs and rocks and look down before you step over them, and don't stick your hands or fingers in places you cannot see.

Rattlesnakes hunt on warm evenings, so do not walk around at night without a flashlight if the weather is warm. And be careful walking on roads on summer nights. Snakes like to come out and heat themselves on the warm blacktop after dark. To help protect yourself from snakebites, wear hiking boots that go over your ankles. You can also wear *gaiters*, which are strong pieces of material that wrap around your legs from your shoes to your knees.

Keep your dog close to you whenever you're in an area where snakes can be found. Dogs frequently stick their noses very close to rattlesnakes in order to sniff and investigate them. If you live in snake country, consider getting a rattlesnake vaccine for your dog.

If you encounter a dead venomous snake, *don't touch it*. A snake's nervous system remains active and can cause the snake's mouth to bite long after the snake is dead. If you want the rattle off a dead rattlesnake, first chop off the snake's head and bury it, *without touching it*.

If a snake does bite you, try not to get upset. The first thing you should do is check to see whether it is actually one of the venomous varieties. I have seen people who should have known better become hysterical because they were bitten by a harmless gopher snake. In addition, doctors and medical personnel will want to know what kind of snake it was.

If you are bitten by a nonvenomous snake, clean and bandage the wound. (See chapter 11, p. 177, for information on first-aid procedures.) If you are bitten by a venomous snake, that's a scary situation, especially if you are far from a hospital. But don't panic; although approximately 8,000 people get bitten by venomous snakes every year in the United States, only about 15 victims die. In addition, keep in mind that about one in four snakebites made by venomous snakes is a *dry bite*, meaning that the snake failed to inject its dangerous venom into your body. If, on the other hand, you do get a dose of venom, you may experience the following symptoms:

- Redness and swelling in the bite area
- Severe pain
- Nausea and dizziness
- Trouble breathing
- Sweating
- Increased saliva
- Thirst
- Fever
- Numbness
- Tingling in the face or body
- Changes in vision

If you have any of these symptoms, you need to have someone take you to a hospital for antivenom shots as soon as possible. In the meantime, get away from the snake, and try to stay calm. Yes, I know—it's hard to stay calm after being bitten by a rattlesnake, especially if you're all alone and lost in the wilderness. Still, the more you get excited or run around, the faster the venom will travel through your body, so just try to keep as still as possible. Keep the bitten area still, if necessary creating a splint to immobilize it, just as you would for a broken bone (see chapter 11, p. 185). If possible, lie down or keep the area of your body that was bitten positioned so that it is at the same level as or lower than your heart. The area will probably swell quickly.

Snakebite experts recommend that you follow these additional guidelines:

- Remove jewelry near the bite site immediately
- Take off tight-fitting clothes near the bite site
- *Do not* apply ice to the bite area
- *Do not* take pain-relief medication
- *Do not* cut across the fang marks and try to suck out the poison
- *Do not* apply a tourniquet to stop the flow of blood in the bite area
- Get to a hospital as soon as possible

Again—prevention is the key. If you stay aware of where you're putting your feet and hands, you can almost always avoid getting bitten in the first place.

OTHER CREATURES

Some other potentially dangerous animals you may encounter in the wilderness include:

- **Alligators.** They used to be rare in the United States, but now alligators are fairly common in swampy areas of the southeast. Like lots of other critters, they are most active in the evening and at night. Most of the advice about alligators is pretty simple and not terribly surprising: if you're in alligator country, don't swim in or camp near water,

don't put your hands or legs over the side of a boat, and don't throw food or fish into the water. If you find yourself facing an alligator, get away from it. Fast. When alligators attack on land, they usually make one grab at you; if they miss, you are usually safe.

- **Snapping turtles.** Snapping turtles are the largest of all freshwater turtles. They are found across the United States from Maine to the Rocky Mountains. Their heads and necks are highly flexible, and they can turn and bite almost to their tails. One type found mainly in the southeastern states, called the alligator snapping turtle, can easily weigh over 100 pounds, and it has powerful jaws that can bite off a finger. Experts say that snapping turtles are curious and not overly aggressive but do not like to be bothered by humans. They lie at the bottoms of muddy or slow-moving rivers or ponds, waiting to catch fish or water birds that come near. On land, a snapping turtle bites not to feed but to defend itself, and it will hold on to whatever it has bitten and not let go. If it's killed, it will hold on even after death, but a live turtle will let go if it's placed in the water. You should not wade or swim in muddy areas where these turtles live.

- **Toads**. Many species of toads are poisonous to both humans and other animals, including dogs. It's a good idea to just steer clear of toads. If you do come into contact with one, always wash your hands, and be sure not to put your fingers in your mouth or near your eyes until you do. Don't ever try to eat a toad, either—even after it's cooked, its poisons are still very harmful. How do you tell the difference between a toad and a frog? Toads have stubbier bodies and dry, bumpy skin, while frogs' skin is smooth and wet. In addition, toads usually walk instead of hopping, so their hind legs are shorter than those of a frog.

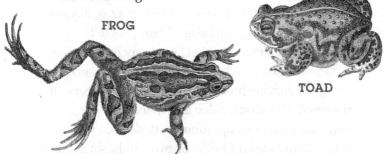

FROG

TOAD

- **Skunks**. I love skunks. I also hate them. These little stinkers are found everywhere in the United States and in most of Canada, often in city suburbs. My car, my house, and my dog have been decontaminated three times after skunk invasions. When a skunk feels threatened, it sprays foul-smelling chemicals at the threat. The smell is so bad that it makes humans

sick and gives them headaches and sore throats. Dogs that are sprayed in the face may foam at the mouth. Skunks can also carry rabies. Needless to say, you should avoid them—and keep your pets away from them as well! Dogs are the main targets of skunks, and unless you surprise or scare one, you will probably not be directly sprayed—but because skunks spray up to 10 feet away, anyone or anything nearby will be hit. Many people have heard that you can get rid of skunk smell by bathing in tomato juice, but that isn't true. Instead, you can buy great enzyme products that remove the worst of the smell. If you own a dog and share your neighborhood or campground with skunks, you might want to keep a bottle or two handy, since skunk sprayings usually occur in the middle of the night, when pet stores are closed. If you do not have any on hand, white vinegar also helps wash away the smell. So does a shampoo of a quart of hydrogen peroxide, ¼ cup of baking soda, and a squirt of dish soap. Keep the mixture on for five minutes, then rinse thoroughly; it must be kept away from noses and

eyes. No matter what remedy you try, you probably
will not be able to remove a skunk's odor completely,
even with multiple remedies. Time is the only real
cure—after one memorable dosing, my dog smelled
like skunk for more than a year.

- **Raccoons.** These cute and clever creatures are not
  usually a threat to you, although older raccoons can
  be quite large and ill-tempered. Raccoons can
  also carry rabies, and they will certainly bite if they're
  cornered. They will also fight with your dog, steal
  all your food, and then climb up a tree and call you
  bad names in raccoon language. See the section on
  bears (p. 83) to learn how to safeguard your food
  from these camp thieves.

- **Bats.** These flying mammals are commonly seen after
  dark. Many people think that bats deliberately fly into
  people's hair. That isn't true, but they will fly near
  you to eat the
  mosquitoes
  that are hovering

around you. Each bat eats hundreds of bugs each
night, so they are valuable to have around. (Without
animals like bats and birds, there would be so
many mosquitoes and other flying bugs around
that we wouldn't even be able to go outside.)
However, bats can carry rabies, and their droppings
contain a dangerous, disease-causing fungus called
histoplasmosis. Spores from this fungus can float in
the air you breathe, so it's a good idea to stay out
of caves or buildings that contain lots of bats. And you
should never touch a bat unless you are wearing gloves.

- **Rodents.** In the woods and deserts of the United
  States—particularly in caves and deserted old
  buildings—you will find deer mice, cute little things
  with big eyes and ears. Unfortunately, some of them
  carry *hantavirus*, a flu-like disease that can kill you.
  In addition, both mice and rats can transmit
  leptospirosis and other dangerous diseases to humans
  and other animals, including dogs. Be careful about
  taking shelter anyplace that has mouse or rat
  droppings or nests. Squirrels and chipmunks have

RAT

fleas that can be infected with disease. Avoid all rodents and try not to handle anything, like firewood, that has been used as a rodent nest.

MOUSE

Because North America is so huge and its animal population is so varied, I have not written about every single dangerous creature you might meet. To be prepared, you need to learn about your area and the animals that live in it. A hiker in New York needs to be extra careful not to step on a copperhead hidden in the leaves but probably doesn't have to check behind him or her for a stalking mountain lion. In western states, a slippery rock may be the most dangerous thing you will encounter in the water—people wade and swim without a thought—while in other parts of the country, like Louisiana or Florida, the water is home to cottonmouths, alligators, snapping turtles, and other dangerous animals.

You can find lots of information on the animals in your area at your local bookstore or library and on the Internet. See the resources section (p. 207) for a list of especially helpful websites.

7

GETTING THE BEST OF BUGS

Although most people are fearful of bears and cougars, some tiny bugs are actually much more dangerous, because of the diseases they can carry. However, there is no reason to be scared to death of every bug you see. After reading this chapter, you should know which ones to admire and which to avoid.

MOSQUITOES

These annoying creatures not only bite you and leave you covered with itchy spots; they carry diseases as well. In the United States, mosquitoes can be infected with West Nile virus and several types of encephalitis. Once during a late-winter training session, a search and rescue dog handler and I were absolutely covered with biting mosquitoes. Within days, we both became ill with severe flu-like symptoms, and it took over a year for us to recover.

Fortunately, mosquito-carried illnesses in North America are rare. Encephalitis is most commonly found in Texas, Louisiana, Alabama, Mississippi, California, Colorado,

Kansas, Illinois, Ohio, Indiana, Tennessee, Florida, New Jersey, and Canada. West Nile virus is found mostly in Texas, California, Colorado, and Canada. Regardless of where you live, you are bound to be bitten by mosquitoes now and then, but never fear—if you use insect repellent, your risk of disease is practically nonexistent.

You should carry the repellent in your pack (see chapter 12, p. 197) and use it whenever mosquitoes are around. If you have no repellent, cover yourself with extra clothing or a tarp and put a layer of mud on body areas that are exposed. (Native people have used mud or plants such as daisies, mint, lavender, eucalyptus, yarrow, and sagebrush to keep mosquitoes away for hundreds of years.) Smart hikers also carry a square of mosquito netting to put over their head to protect themselves from swarms of mosquitoes. Make sure that your first-aid kit (which you should always have with you when you're exploring the wilderness) contains hydrocortisone cream, which you can use to lessen the itching, redness, and swelling from mosquito or other insect bites.(For more information on first-aid kits, see chapter 12, p. 201.)

For some reason, according to scientists, these little bloodsuckers seem to prefer certain people. They're also attracted to dark colors; they're less likely to land on you if your clothes are light brown or khaki colored. Although they are most active in the evening, they are often found during the day in shady areas, especially those near water. Some people are highly allergic to mosquito bites and may experience bruising at bite sites, hives, or asthma symptoms after being bitten. For those people who have trouble breathing after being bitten, repellent and the proper clothing are essential. In addition, allergy doctors can test you for "skeeter syndrome" and prescribe medication if it turns out you are allergic to mosquitoes.

TICKS

No one likes ticks. They are found in rural areas everywhere in the continental United States except at the highest altitudes. Some ticks are about the size of sesame seeds and are very hard to see. They have tiny heads, large bodies, and eight legs. They attach themselves to humans and animals, suck their blood, and then drop off to lay eggs and make more ticks. They can infect people with 11 different diseases, including Rocky Mountain spotted fever, relapsing fever, anaplasmosis, and Lyme disease. Several of these diseases are relatively common. Each year, between 20,000 and 30,000 people are infected with Lyme disease in the United States due to tick bites. Dogs that are bitten by ticks can also become infected with Lyme disease.

actual size of   tick that's
many ticks   full of blood

You can help to keep ticks off you by spraying your clothing with insect repellent; by wearing a hat, long pants, and long sleeves; and by tucking your pant legs into your hiking boots. Your dog needs insect repellent, too; there are specialized products available at your pet store to repel and kill mosquitoes, fleas, and ticks. Do not use your insect repellent on your pet!

Ticks like grassy, wooded areas with bushes, and they are commonly found in places where deer have made beds in the leaves and grass (they feed on deer blood). They are most active during summer months. To help avoid ticks when you're out exploring, stay in the center of the trail and try not to brush against bushes or grasses. People often pick up ticks by sitting on logs or stumps, so check before you sit. After your hike, inspect yourself, your companions, and your dog for ticks. Be sure to look inside and behind ears, in the hair, under arms, behind knees, and around the waist.

Despite what some people believe, you should never use a lit match or petroleum jelly (Vaseline) to remove a tick. This will stimulate the tick to inject more of its saliva into you, which could make you sicker. Instead, remove it by hand—be sure to wear gloves or cover your fingers with a tissue—or use tweezers. Grab the tick close to your skin and pull it up and away from your skin slowly. Do not twist it. Or you can use a tick extractor, which is a little metal tool made just for removing ticks; I carry one on my day pack. Clean the area with antiseptic after you have removed and killed the tick.

If you feel sick days or weeks after you have been bitten by a tick, see your doctor as soon as possible. There are medicines for tick diseases, but they work best if you take them soon after you feel sick.

CHIGGERS

Chiggers are very tiny red mites that can bite you and cause terrible itching. They do not burrow into the skin, as many people think; instead, they crawl into your clothing and bite your skin. To keep them off you, use insect repellent, and tuck your pants into boots or socks. Chiggers are usually found in hot and damp areas, such as the southern and eastern parts of the United States; they're rarely found in desert or mountain regions.

ANTS

Most ants are harmless. However, if you live where there are fire ants or red harvester ants, you already know just how bad a few ants can be. These insects attack and repeatedly sting pets, people, birds, and any other animal that crosses their path. When they sting you, they inject poison that makes your skin feel like it is on fire. The poison usually causes blisters to appear on your skin, and for the rare person who's allergic, even one bite can result in breathing problems and other serious medical issues.

Although fire ants are not native to the United States— they were brought here accidentally by South American ships in the 1930s—they are spreading rapidly across the country. Several types of fire ants are found across the southern half of the United States and in both the western and eastern coastal areas. These reddish-brown bugs prefer suburban neighborhoods with cleared ground—they can often be seen crawling out of a mound of dirt with nothing growing around it—but they can be found in all kinds of places, including under rocks or logs. Fire ants climb into peoples' clothes and sting them repeatedly. They also get between dogs' toes and sting them over and over.

Fire ant stings need to be washed to remove any poison that's on the skin. Use cold water to help keep the swelling down and cover the bites with hydrocortisone cream.

Red harvester ants can both sting and bite you. They are also reddish in color and they live in holes around which all the grass and plants have been removed and eaten by the ants.

Cow killers, or velvet ants, look like large, fuzzy ants, but they are actually wasps. They are found across the United States and Canada and live mostly in areas with sandy soil. Cow killers are usually red, yellow, or orange,

but some of them are black or striped. The females don't have wings; they live on the ground. A velvet ant can give you a really painful sting— some people claim that it's so painful it could kill a cow. In fact, it's said that the velvet ant has the most painful sting of any insect in North America—but I don't want to find out if that is true!

The key to avoiding ant and cow killer attacks is simply to leave them alone. Before you build a shelter, always check the area carefully for signs of the critters described above. If you're in an area of the country that has fire ants, red harvester ants, or cow killers, be especially alert, and if you find any, *move somewhere else*, where you do not see any ants on the ground.

BEES AND WASPS

HONEY BEE

Just about everyone has heard of "killer bees," which is the common name for Africanized honeybees. They are now found across the southern United States from Louisiana to California, and they are spreading north. Regular, non-Africanized honeybees usually sting only in self-defense—when they're swatted, stepped on, or accidentally swallowed, or when a person gets too close to their hive—but killer bees will attack people or pets for no apparent reason at all. You cannot tell the difference between killer bees and "normal" bees by looking at them, so it's best to just avoid all beehives and to leave the area if you see or hear more than a few bees, especially if you live in Texas, California, Arizona, or New Mexico. Also, be careful when you're outside drinking soda from a can; bees are attracted to the sugar

WASP

and moisture of soda, and they have been known to crawl inside cans. You don't want to accidentally drink a live bee.

If you are attacked by a swarm of bees, run! Bees will follow you only so far, so keep running until they stop chasing you or until you get into a shelter, such as a house or a car. Experts say *not* to jump into a pool, a lake, or some other watery refuge to escape, because the bees may wait and attack you when you come up for air. Bees are drawn to movement, so don't swat at them. In addition, when they're killed they release a scent that brings even more angry bees. Just get away as fast as possible.

Some types of bees have barbed stingers that break off when they sting you. As soon as you are safe, remove any stingers you find. Be careful not to squeeze the stinger; if you do, it will inject more bee venom into your skin. 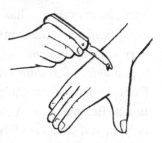 Use something flat, such as a key, the backside of a knife, or the side of a compass, to gently scrape off the stingers. Ice packs or cold cloths will help reduce pain and swelling. If you don't have either of those, you can hold the sting site underwater or cover it with cool mud. Hydrocortisone cream can help as well.

About 1 out of 100 people are very allergic to bee stings and can get very sick or even die from as little as one sting. Even if you aren't allergic to them, you could have trouble breathing if you are stung in the mouth or nose. It is a good idea to carry antihistamine medicine (such as Benadryl) in your first-aid kit to protect against such reactions. If you are allergic to bee stings, be sure to bring along an EpiPen as well. (See chapter 12, p. 202, for more information.)

Unlike bees, wasps do not feed on flower nectar and pollen or produce honey. They nest in trees, old buildings, and in the ground, and they may attack if you get too close to their nest. They do not lose their stingers and can sting repeatedly. The most aggressive type of wasp is called the *yellow jacket*. Yellow jackets are attracted to humans' food, especially meat, and are often bothersome at campground cookouts. The same methods that you use to protect yourselves from bees will also work with wasps.

KISSING BUGS

Kissing bugs are found in almost half of the United States, most commonly in the warmer areas. These winged, beetle-like insects, which are also known as conenoses, bite at night and suck your blood. They are brown or black in color and are less than an inch long. They are often found near rodents' nests—which is one more reason not to sleep near mice or rats.

Kissing bugs belong to a group of insects called *assassin bugs*. Their bites often cause reactions that range from itchy welts on the body or face to a swollen tongue and trouble breathing. A small group of people experience severe, life-threatening allergic reactions to assassin bug bites. Also, in many cases, people who are bitten by assassin bugs more than once experience more severe reactions after the later bites. In California and some areas of the southwestern United States, these bugs carry a deadly disease called Chagas' disease. See your doctor if you are bitten by any type of assassin bug.

There are other species of assassin bugs that look similar in shape to kissing bugs but have orange dots on their wings. They do not feed on animal or human blood.

SCORPIONS

Scorpions can be found in any type of terrain throughout every part of the United States except Alaska. They have eight legs, as well as two front pincers that they use to grab things, and a long, thick tail with a stinger on the end. There are many different kinds, but only one species, the Arizona bark scorpion, is considered dangerous, and it only lives in the southwestern deserts. Bark scorpions have few distinguishing marks, and they can range in color from medium brown to light brown to yellowish brown. I have a friend who was stung by one; he lost all feeling in his finger for a year. Because hospitals now have antivenom medicine to treat scorpion stings, no one in the United States who has been stung in the past few years has died.

All scorpions will sting if provoked. They live under rocks and in rotted logs, so be careful when gathering firewood. They usually emerge from their homes only at night, and when they do, they've been known to crawl inside people's shoes while they're sleeping. Whenever you're in the wilderness, be sure to check your shoes carefully and shake them before you put them on in the morning.

Scorpion stings should be treated in the same way as bee stings (see p. 114): scrape off the stinger, if there is one, and apply ice or cold water to the sting area. If you're stung by a scorpion and you begin to have trouble breathing, are in extreme pain, or experience sensations that feel like electrical jolts at the site of the sting, get to a hospital as soon as you possibly can.

All scorpions glow under UV (ultraviolet) light. Scorpion hunters use UV lights to find and capture specimens to add to their collections. In desert areas, scorpions' homes are easy to find: look for very small openings in the ground that are more wide than tall. Some of the largest scorpions, which are five to six inches long, have the least toxic venom; they can live for over 20 years.

SPIDERS

More than 2,000 people report venomous spider bites to poison control centers in the United States every year, but only about four Americans are killed by spider bites each year. Although many spiders have painful bites, there are four truly dangerous spiders to watch out for:

- **Black widows.** Mature female black widow spiders  are black and shiny, and their round undersides have a distinctive hourglass-shaped marking that is usually red, yellow or orange. This marking is usually solid in color, but some black widows have just a colored outline of an hourglass instead. Not all black widows are actually black; males and immature females can be either black or brown and may have yellow, orange, or white stripes and spots on their backs. A black widow's web is very strong, sticky, and rough-feeling, with no real pattern. Once you touch one, you will always be able to recognize webs made by black widows; they feel like no other spiderweb. Black widows are found throughout the continental United States and southern Canada. During the day, they often hide under rocks, bushes, and logs and in dark, cool buildings—particularly buildings that are home to plenty of insects. Many serious bites have occurred in outhouses. If you use an outhouse while you're camping, be sure to check under the seat before you sit down. Like scorpions, black widows also like to hide in shoes that have been left outside. Whenever you're in the wilderness, be sure to shake your shoes and check them carefully for spiders or other critters before putting them on. If you are bitten by a black widow, there is a chance that you might not develop any symptoms. However, the venom can create severe and painful muscle cramps. Young children may be affected especially strongly.

- **Brown widows**. These relatives of black widows are also venomous. They are not native to the United States, but they began to appear in various places of the country in 2000. Today, brown widows can be found throughout the southern United States from the Gulf Coast to California. Brown widow spiders can be very hard to identify, because they come in many different colors. Their round bodies can range from dark brown to tan, and their mottled markings may be white, black, yellow, brown, or orange. Like black widows, the brown widow has an hourglass-shaped marking on its underside; this marking can be almost any color. The egg sacs of brown widows are very unusual looking: they are round and have little spikes all over them. Some experts say that brown widows are not as dangerous as black widows, but others disagree.

- **Brown recluse spiders**. These small spiders live mostly in the midwestern United States. They are also called violin spiders, because of the violin-shaped markings often found on the tops of their bodies. Although not all brown recluse spiders have the distinctive violin marking, all of them are small in size, with brown bodies and lighter-colored legs. If you cannot tell a violin spider from about six other kinds of small brown spiders, you are not alone; just leave them all alone.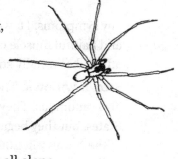

- **Hobo spiders.** Hobo spider bites are often mistakenly thought to be bites from brown recluse spiders, because the bite wounds of each spider look very similar. Hobo spiders live predominantly in the western part of the United States, but they are spreading across the rest of the country and Canada. They are small-to-medium-size, brown, hairy spiders that spin funnel-shaped webs, then hide at the bottom of their funnels to wait for insects to fly into them and become trapped.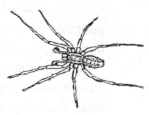

Always be on the lookout for these types of spiders when you're building a shelter, gathering wood, or using an outhouse. A bite by any one of them may harm you. One of my neighbors was bitten by a black widow, and she described it as the most painful experience of her life. Since it is not always possible to identify a poisonous spider by sight, you should always seek medical help if you experience a bite that hurts or doesn't heal or if you feel sick after you've been bitten. You may not even know you have been bitten when it happens, but you will usually feel some pain or itching soon after. Some time after you're bitten by a black widow or a brown widow, for instance, you will feel sick to your stomach, develop a headache and a fever, and feel terrible back or stomach pain. You will need antivenom from a doctor. Put cold water on the bite until you can get to a hospital.

On the other hand, some spiders seem a lot more threatening than they really are. Tarantulas, for example, are large, hairy, and scary looking, but they are not venomous. Although they will bite if provoked, they are usually quite docile. When I lived in New Mexico, I once saw hundreds and hundreds of them running through the grass and sagebrush during their mating season. It was a sight I will never forget.

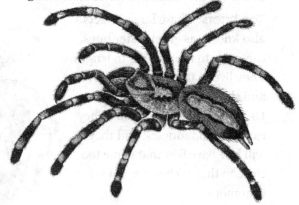

OTHER BUGS

Several other common types of bugs can be unpleasant to encounter:

- **Centipedes**. Centipedes are large, long bugs with plates on the top portions of their bodies and many legs. They will bite if provoked; although centipedes are not venomous, their bite is about as painful as a bee sting. Centipedes hide under damp wood and moss. Due to their armor, they are very hard to kill. Although they can be frightening (I once found one in my house that was about eight inches long), they are not dangerous. They are found everywhere in the United States and Canada, although the giant versions live mostly in the warmer southern and desert states.

- **Toe biters**. These large insects, also known as giant water bugs, can grow to four inches in length. They live at the bottoms of ponds and slow streams across the United States and Canada. They eat fish and tadpoles, and they will bite bare feet that come too close to them. They are not venomous.

- **Biting flies.** Several species of flies, including horseflies, deerflies, biting midges (also called no-see-ums), and gnats, live on the blood of humans and animals. These insects are found almost everywhere, and their bites are painful and can cause allergic reactions in some people. I have been bitten by large horseflies many times, and I can assure you that it really hurts. Most flies that bite do so only during the day. If you're out in the wilderness while these bothersome pests are around, wear a hat and clothing that covers your arms and legs, and use insect repellent to keep them away. You might want to carry a piece of mosquito netting that you can use to cover your head if these insects are really making your life miserable.

DEALING WITH EXTREME WEATHER

When they think of the wilderness dangers that are most likely to hurt or even kill them, most people instantly picture bears, mountain lions, or rattlesnakes. The truth is, the biggest threats in the outdoors come from falling, drowning—and extreme weather. Without proper shelter and supplies, extremes of heat or cold can be more dangerous than a tent full of bears.

HYPOTHERMIA

Cold temperatures can cause *hypothermia* in a surprisingly short amount of time. Hypothermia means that your body temperature has dropped a few degrees below normal, which is around 98.6 degrees Fahrenheit. Mild hypothermia can be fixed, but severe hypothermia is deadly.

Just how do you become hypothermic? There are many ways to lose body heat. As mentioned in chapter 2 (p. 20), sitting or resting on cold ground will pull body heat out of you. Sweating from exercise in cold weather also cools down your body quickly. Being exposed to cold wind or breathing in cold air can also quickly cool you.

The first signs of hypothermia are usually goose bumps and shivering. Shivering is actually your body's way of trying to create heat by moving your muscles. You may shiver just a little bit, or as your body becomes colder, you may shake all over. Your skin might turn red, as though you have a sunburn. You may also find that you can't quickly touch your thumb to your little finger. You may experience the *umbles*: stumbles, mumbles, fumbles, bumbles, and tumbles—in other words, you may become clumsy, have trouble speaking or walking, trip and fall, or become confused and unable to take care of tasks. You may also feel sleepy, have no energy, or start thinking that you don't care what happens to you or that you just want to be left alone. If you find yourself suffering from any of these symptoms—even shivering—take action immediately! You must change your situation and get warm and active right away.

If your hypothermia grows more severe, you will become pale and your fingers, toes, ears, or lips might start to turn blue. As your body chills, your heart, brain, and lungs will struggle to work. You will become confused and foggy. If your situation is not fixed soon, you will die.

Because hypothermia causes confusion and sluggishness, you need to be alert and watch yourself and others for the symptoms so you can take immediate action. One early spring day, my search dog in training had to pass a swimming test. He hated swimming and I absolutely could not convince him to jump in the water. Finally, I swam out into the cold mountain lake myself, then called him to swim to me. He did, but when he reached me, he tried to get out of the water by climbing onto my head. He was a very large dog, and I ended up completely underwater. I also lost my car keys. By the time I finally located and retrieved my keys, I had been submerged in cold water for over 20 minutes. Weirdly enough, at some point I had stopped shivering, and I was actually feeling warm in the water. I wasn't really warm, though—I was hypothermic. Fortunately, I was surrounded by lots of knowledgeable search and rescue people who knew the signs of hypothermia. They insisted that I put on dry clothes right away. Once I warmed up, I was just fine.

To keep yourself warm and safe, follow these tips:

- **Wear multiple layers of loose clothing**. If you wear two or three layers of loose clothing, air is able to flow between the layers. The air helps insulate your body and keeps you much warmer than one thick layer of clothing can.

- **Avoid clothing that's made of cotton**. There is a saying in the world of survival: "Cotton kills." When cotton gets wet in cold weather, it takes a long time to dry and pulls a lot of heat out of your body. If you are wearing cotton in the rain or snow, you risk becoming chilled in a very short amount of time. Polyester fleece clothing holds in body heat and insulates you from the cold, and down-filled jackets are wonderful for protecting you in cold, dry weather.

- **Keep your head, neck, and hands covered.**
  This is such simple but such important advice. You
  lose most of your body heat through your head and
  neck. A knit or fleece hat weighs next to nothing, but
  it can save your life. Be sure to keep your ears
  covered. And your mom is right: you need to put on
  your gloves. Always carry a pair of gloves or mittens
  in your pack so you can protect your hands from the
  cold. (If you have a spare pair of socks, you can use
  them as mittens as well.)

- **Keep your clothes dry.** Damp clothing cools off
  your body. If you find yourself in wet weather and
  you have no waterproof clothing to wear as a top
  layer, you can cover yourself with a trash bag to stay
  dry. Use small bags over your hands, too, to keep
  them dry. If your clothes do get wet, build a fire as
  soon as possible so that you can warm yourself and
  dry your clothes.

- **Don't wear clothing that causes you to sweat or
  become overheated.** Clothes absorb sweat and
  become damp. When you are walking fast, building
  a shelter, or hauling wood in cold weather, take
  off your jacket or outer layer of clothing so you don't
  sweat, then put it back on after you are finished
  working or exercising. (That's another good reason to
  dress in layers.)

- **Protect yourself from the wind.** *Windchill* is a
  term that describes how cold the temperature outside

feels to people and animals when the cooling effects of wind are taken into account. Wind pulls heat from your body—that's why you feel colder on days when it is both cold and windy than on days when it is just as cold but not windy. Just by finding shelter and getting out of the wind, you will be warmer.

- **Eat foods that contain a lot of calories.** Calories give you energy, and energy helps to keep you warm. Be sure to bring along easy-to-carry high-calorie foods such chocolate, peanuts, or almonds whenever you head out to explore the wilderness.

- **Get active.** Run in place, do jumping jacks, or exercise in some other way to help your blood circulate in your body and keep you warm. Swing your arms around now and then to keep the blood flowing to your hands. Remember to take off a layer or two of clothing so that you do not sweat while you're exercising. When you've finished, put the clothing back on.

- **Insulate yourself.** If you are cold, stuff your clothing with pine needles, dry leaves, or anything else that will help to insulate your body from cold temperatures and wind. A layer of leaves between your shirt and jacket will help keep you warm. You could also wear a trash bag as an outer layer of "clothing" and stuff pine needles or grass between the bag and your real clothes.

- **Use disposable heat packs.** Chemically activated heat packs with sticky backing can be lifesavers. Stick them on your skin in areas where your blood flows closest to the surface—such as hands, neck, underarms, feet, or groin. The heat from these packs will last for hours.

- **Drink lots of fluids.** When you are dehydrated, your blood does not flow as well as it should and you become colder faster. You can help to keep your body warm by drinking plenty of water—preferably warm water, but cold water is better than no water at all. Warm sugared drinks are even better at helping you to stay warm because they give you calories as well. Some people carry hot chocolate mix that they can use with water when they hike in the winter months. If you have a package of powdered gelatin that contains sugar, you can dissolve some of it in hot water and drink it. Whatever your source of fluids, be sure to keep drinking throughout the night when it's cold outside—even when you're tucked into your shelter. You may think it's a better idea to stop drinking so you don't have to go out into the cold to pee, but you'll actually stay much warmer if keep yourself well hydrated.

- **Take advantage of your buddy's body warmth.** Huddle with another person or with your dog, preferably underneath a Mylar-lined tarp. (Dogs are nature's electric blankets!)

- **Light a fire.** Obviously, a campfire can help to keep you warm.

If you have become hypothermic, try to heat yourself *gradually*. Since hypothermia means that your body temperature has dropped several degrees, if you bring the temperature up too quickly, it can be a shock to your system. For example, don't jump right into a hot car wrapped in multiple blankets with heat packs stuck all over your body. Instead, just sit next to a fire with a blanket and some heat packs.

FROSTBITE

Frostbite occurs when the skin or other tissues in a particular part of the body actually freeze. Frostbite can be mild or severe, depending on how frozen the area becomes. You are most likely to get frostbite on your feet, hands, ears, nose, or face. Be on the lookout for these telltale signs of frostbite:

- An area of your skin becomes white or grayish in color

- You experience a "pins and needles" feeling, then numbness, in the frostbitten area

- The area aches or throbs with pain.

- If the area feels "like a block of wood"—in other words, if you can't feel anything there—and the flesh looks pale and hard, you have *severe frostbite*; the tissue has frozen completely.

One of the biggest survival myths says that if a person has frostbite, you should rub his or her frozen body parts with snow. *Never do that*, and never let anyone do it to you. Rubbing ice on frozen tissue will cause more damage. It is a horrible idea. In fact, it's a bad idea to rub frostbitten body parts with *anything*.

As soon as you see or feel any of the early signs of frostbite, start moving and warming that area of your body. Clench your fists and wiggle your toes, if those areas are starting to feel tingly or achy. If you think you feel signs of frostbite in your face, scrunch up your face, make funny faces, and do anything else you can think of to warm it up. Take your hands out of your gloves or mittens and cover your ears or nose with your warm hands. If your fingers start to hurt, tuck your bare hands inside your jacket and under your armpits to warm them up. If you are with a buddy, take turns looking at each other's face and ears for signs of frostbite. By keeping your skin warm and the blood circulating, you can stop frostbite from setting in.

But once you've developed severe frostbite, the worst thing you can do is to thaw (or unfreeze) the frostbitten skin, have it freeze again, and rewarm it. What does this mean if you are out in the wild and frostbitten? Unless you know for sure that you can get to a hospital right away or that you can keep yourself warm and dry in your shelter until you are rescued, do not thaw or warm areas of the body that you know are severely frostbitten. It is better to live with frostbite and wait for medical help than it is to unfreeze the frozen skin only to have it refreeze.

If you are someplace warm and dry and you can stay there, soak the frozen part in slightly warm water. (Be prepared to experience a lot of pain—it really hurts to thaw or warm frozen skin.) And, of course, get to a hospital as soon as you can. The best way to deal with frostbite is to not to let it happen in the first place. Protect yourself from even the first signs of frostbite at all times. If this means you have to keep moving and exercising all night to keep warm, then do it.

HEAT ILLNESS

Let's say that you are lost or just exploring the wilderness. You brought water with you but you don't have much left. Your mouth is dry, you are starting to get cramps in your legs, and you feel sick to your stomach. Should you sit down and drink some of your remaining water? Yes! You are showing signs of dehydration and heat exhaustion.

Heat exhaustion can be mildly uncomfortable, but it can quickly turn into a fatal condition called *heat stroke*. The symptoms of heat exhaustion are:

- Tiredness or weakness
- Feeling dizzy or sick to your stomach
- Fainting
- Heavy sweating
- Fever
- Headaches

- Muscle cramps
- Dark urine or inability to pee
- Cool, damp skin

If you have any of these signs, you need to cool your body immediately. Get in the shade, or better yet, some cool water. Drink lots of fluids, especially water, even if you do not feel thirsty. If you are wearing heavy or tight clothes, remove or loosen them. If you can wet the clothes you're still wearing, do so; the fastest way to cool your body is to wear wet clothes. Because the ground is *much* cooler under the surface, if you have the energy, dig down a little to cooler ground in the shade. Even a few inches down, the ground is many degrees cooler than the surface. Lie down in the shade with your feet propped up slightly higher than your head. Rest. Do not do anything physical until all the symptoms have gone away.

For survival purposes, it's better to wear lightweight, loose-fitting long pants and a lightweight long-sleeved shirt in the heat than shorts and a tank top. You do not want the sun to shine directly on your skin and cause it to heat up or become sunburned. In very hot climates, cotton clothing is better than clothing made from a synthetic such as polyester, because it allows for better air circulation. Remember, "cotton kills" in cold weather, but it helps to keep you cool in hot weather.

Another easy way to help yourself stay cool is to wear a hat. When your head heats up, so does the rest of you. However, a regular baseball cap is not a great hat to wear in a hot area. Baseball caps hold the heat inside them, next to your head. A better choice is a lightweight cowboy hat or a hat that has a wide, lightweight brim and mesh or mosquito netting around the crown that allow air to circulate beneath the hat. There are even hats with cooling pads that are made to be dipped into water regularly.

You can also wet a bandanna and use it to cool your neck. Some people who have become lost and who did not have a good supply of water have even peed on their bandannas, waved them around to cool them off, and used them to cool their skin. How about making a hat out of your bandanna, or using your tarp and a couple of sticks to make an umbrella? Do whatever you can to stay out of the sun and keep your head cool.

SUN OR SNOW BLINDNESS

When UV (ultraviolet) rays from the sun are reflected into your eyes for hours, it can actually sunburn your *corneas*, the transparent layers of tissue that cover the iris and pupil of each eye. People with green or blue eyes are especially at risk, as is anyone who's surrounded by highly reflective surfaces like snow or desert sand.

As you can imagine, burning your corneas hurts. It starts with a scratchy feeling in your eye, like you have dust in it. After a while, you feel real pain and aren't able to open your eyes. If you have a severe case, your eyes could become damaged and you might go temporarily blind. In the wilderness, there's not much you can do to speed up recovery except rest with your eyes closed.

To help prevent eye damage in the first place, wear sunglasses, shade your eyes with a hat, or tie some cloth over your eyes like a blindfold, leaving just a small slit to look out of. You can make eyeshades from bark, plastic, or anything that limits the amount of light that hits your eyes. In highly reflective environments, UV rays can still harm you on a cloudy day, so keep your eyes protected even if the sun is behind clouds.

HOW HOT IS IT? ASK A CRICKET.

A cricket's chirps can tell you the temperature of its surroundings. Count the number of chirps a single cricket makes in 15 seconds and add 40 to the sum—that's the approximate temperature in degrees Fahrenheit. For instance, if a cricket makes 38 chirps in 15 seconds, it is about 78 degrees Fahrenheit.

FINDING FOOD

Let's get real here. If you get lost in the wilderness, you will not be spending much time searching for food. You will be busy finding shelter and water, then signaling for help from search and rescue. It is great to know how to survive by foraging for edible plants or trapping and killing wild game, but it is much smarter to bring food with you. Some good choices are jerky, trail mix, dehydrated backpacker meals, or MREs (meals ready to eat).

MREs were created to provide full meals to soldiers in combat in the 1980s, to replace the awful-tasting ration meals used since World War II. Military supply stores and Internet sites carry civilian versions of MREs that stay edible for years as long as they're unopened. More than 20 different kinds of MREs are available—there are even vegetarian MREs—and each one includes a main course, a side dish, crackers, drink mix, condiments, and dessert. Outdoor supply stores also carry terrific meals that heat themselves by a chemical process when you pull a tab on the package. They also offer a good selection of lightweight dehydrated meals, from plain macaroni and cheese to exotic Thai dishes. To prepare dehydrated food to eat, you just pour boiling water right into the food bag.

There are also special food bars that are made for long-term survival. When kept in their original, sealed packages these bars last up to five years. Some have enough calories in each bar to sustain two adults for a day. In an emergency, several bars could feed you for a week.

But what do you do if you become stranded or lost and you don't have any food with you? This chapter explains a few ways to locate food in a survival situation. Remember, though, that you can live for weeks without food if you have to. Before you even consider eating any questionable plant or animal in the wild, ask yourself a simple question: "Is this bit of food worth it? Do I really need it so badly that I'm willing to risk vomiting, getting diarrhea, or becoming really sick?"

> ❌ Ignore the old saying that you can eat any-thing that you see an animal eating. *It is not true*. Bugs can eat mushrooms that are toxic to humans. Goats eat poison oak and other plants that could make you very ill. Little garter snakes can eat poisonous salamanders that would kill a human adult in hours.

PLANTS TO AVOID

In addition to edible plants, the wilderness is filled with all kinds of plants that will make you sick or kill you within a couple of hours after eating them. Poisonous plants often share the same characteristics. ***Do not eat or even touch*** any plant that has:

✖ **Milky sap or sap that changes color when the plant is cut open, such as turning from clear to white**

✖ **Umbrella-shaped clusters of flowers**

✖ **Bulbs that look like garlic or onions**

✖ **Carrot-like roots and leaves**

✖ **Bean-like pods or parts that look like peas**

✖ **Leaves with tiny hairs or fuzz**

✖ **Single berries, especially white, green, yellow, or red ones**

✖ **A smell like almonds**

✖ **Seeds that are purple, black, or pink**

There are entire books written about wild plants. Most have chapters full of information on poisonous plants. Here are just a few of the poisonous plants commonly found in North America:

- **Mushrooms.** Every year across the planet, about 8,000 people are poisoned by eating mushrooms. Most of these people do not die, but many do damage to their kidneys or liver. Many edible mushrooms look almost identical to their poisonous relatives, so you should leave mushroom-gathering to the experts. Some people think that any fungus that grows on a tree is safe to eat (mushrooms are a type of fungus), but this is a myth; there are several kinds of poisonous mushrooms that grow on tree trunks, and they look just like their edible cousins. Even some edible mushrooms can cause illness if they're eaten raw. *Leave all mushrooms and other fungi alone.* Dogs need to be kept away from all fungi, too—many dogs have died after eating poisonous mushrooms. Young puppies and certain breeds of dogs that are adventuresome eaters, such as Labrador retrievers, seem to be especially likely to eat poisonous mushrooms. If you suspect that your dog has eaten any kind of wild mushroom, get him or her to a vet as soon as possible.

- **Death camas.** Also known as black snakeroot, this plant is found across the United States in meadows or natural areas. These sneaky little bulbs not only look just like wild onions, but they also often grow right next to onions. Onion bulbs smell like onions, but death camas do not. They also have slightly different-shaped leaves than onions. Still, most people have a hard time telling a poisonous death camas from an edible onion. The death camas is one of the most poisonous plants in nature, and it is responsible for the deaths of livestock all across the United States. Eating one small bulb or flower can kill you within hours. That's why it's best to avoid *all* onion-type plants.

- **Hemlock**. Hundreds of years ago, this plant was used to poison condemned prisoners. Not only should it should not be eaten, but it shouldn't even be touched. Hemlock is a flowering plant, and its flowers grow in clusters that look like little umbrellas. It grows in damp areas and meadows. The hemlock root looks like a wild carrot or a wild parsnip (which can give you a rash if you touch it), and it's difficult to tell the difference between hemlock and either of its edible relatives. Since there are many plants that look just like it, it is best to avoid all plants that have flower clusters shaped like umbrellas.

- **Pea- or bean-type plants**. Many highly toxic plants have seedpods that look like wild peas or some type of bean. If you see anything that looks like a pea or a bean growing on a plant, just leave that plant alone.

- **Nettles**. Nettles and other plants with hairy or fuzzy leaves can cause stinging burns if you touch them, and some have toxins that can make you sick if you eat them. While nettles can be eaten after they've been boiled in water, it's best to leave them alone. If you are stung by a nettle plant, treat the sting in the same way that you would a bee sting (see chapter 7, p. 114).

- **Berries.** Be very careful about eating berries. Unless you are absolutely certain that they are OK, it's best to leave them alone. A few berries are not worth dying over. Many common plants have poisonous berries, including holly, mistletoe, deadly nightshade, jimson weed, and yews. Most single berries are dangerous

SINGLE BERRIES (not safe)   **AGGREGATE BERRIES (safe)**

to eat, so unless you go blueberry picking regularly and know exactly what to look for, leave the single ones alone. Blueberries taste wonderful, but deadly nightshade plants have dark blue berries too. Especially avoid green, white, or yellow single berries. However, *aggregate berries*, in which each fruit is made up of lots of tiny berries, are edible. Blackberries, raspberries, and thimbleberries (see p. 147) are all aggregate berries.

POISON IVY, POISON OAK, AND POISON SUMAC

Although they look different, all three of these plants are essentially the same in one important respect—they all contain poisonous oils that produce a rash whenever they come in contact with skin. You can be exposed to the oils directly by touching the plant or indirectly by touching something that has brushed against the plant, like a jacket or your dog. Unfortunately, each one of these plants can vary in appearance and can be hard to identify. For instance, a poison oak plant can be a small shrub with bright green leaves in one area, and a tree-size plant with purple and dark green leaves over the next hill.

Poison oak and poison ivy both have glossy leaves that grow in groups of three, which is why there is a rhyme that says, "Leaves of three, let it be."

POISON IVY

Poison ivy is found everywhere in the United States except Alaska, Hawaii, and the western coastal areas. Its greenish leaves can be either tooth-edged (like the teeth of a saw) or smooth. It turns yellow, orange, and red in the fall, and it has white berries in the fall and winter. It can be a small plant, a creeping vine or a giant shrub. Poison oak has oak-like leaves that may be any color of green, yellow, purple,

POISON OAK

red, or orange. It grows in huge bushes and vines all over the west coasts of the United States and Canada except in desert areas. Horses, cows, and goats often eat it without a problem. Its poison does not affect dogs, but dogs that run through poison oak can carry the plant's poisonous oil on their fur and transfer it to humans.

Poison sumac can be harder to avoid than its cousins poison oak or poison ivy, because it matures into a tree that looks nothing like its relatives. It grows in wet areas in the eastern half of the United States. Unlike poison oak and ivy, its leaves are arranged in larger groups, with 7 to 13 smooth leaves on a stem. The leaves turn

POISON SUMAC

orange and red in autumn. In the early fall, poison sumac grows yellow-white berries in hanging bunches. Poison sumac trees can grow to be 20 feet tall.

About 90 percent of people are allergic to poison ivy, oak, and sumac. The more of these plants you touch, the more likely you are to become allergic to them. The rash may appear a few hours or even a day or two after you touch the plant's oils, and it usually lasts a week or so. Your body's reaction can range from itchy red spots to huge blisters and open sores. The rash itself can't be spread, but the poisonous oils that caused it can be transferred to other areas of your body or to other people.

Do not touch any plants that meet the above descriptions (and keep your dog away from them, as well). If you realize that you've come into contact with one of them, your best bet is to wash off the oils with soap as soon as possible. There are also special products you can carry to wash off the poisonous oils; a popular one is called Tecnu. Use cold water—warm water will spread the oils around. If you can go for a swim in a chlorinated pool, the rash will clear up much faster.

Since you probably will be hiking or camping when you come down with the rash, you should keep some hydrocortisone cream in your first-aid kit (see chapter 12, p. 201) to help soothe the itch and calm down your skin's reaction to the poisonous oil. Sometimes cold wet cloths help with the skin irritation, especially if there is swelling.

Be especially careful not to burn any of these plants. Their smoke is toxic, and it can cause severe problems if you inhale it or if it gets in your eyes. If either of these things happens, see a doctor as soon as possible.

EDIBLE PLANTS

The following plants are edible. However, make absolutely sure you've identified a plant correctly before you eat it. If you are not 100 percent sure a plant is safe, *do not touch it.*

- **Pine trees.** *Do not* confuse pines with other trees. Yews, which are poisonous, have small red berries and flat leaves. Cedars and cypress have flattened leaves, and firs have short needles. Pine trees have long needles and pinecones. Pine needles can be crushed and used to make a tea that is high in vitamin C, and the pine tree's tender inner bark can be eaten. And each pinecone holds many pine nuts, each under a different section of the cone. Pine nuts are one of the most nutritious foods found in the forest. They are especially easy to harvest in Jeffrey, piñon, sugar, and grey pines. Each nut is covered by

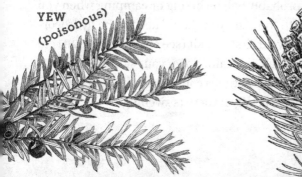

YEW
(poisonous)

PINE
(safe)

a hard shell that needs to removed before the nut can be eaten, much like a sunflower seed. Native people used to heat pinecones to make them open up, remove the pine nuts, and then roast the nuts to make the shells easy to remove. Pine nuts are delicious and full of fat and calories. I taught one of my dogs to get the nuts out of pinecones. She would spend hours in my yard knocking them out of the cones.

- **Blackberries, raspberries, and thimbleberries.** In many areas of the country, from rain forests in the West to very hot, dry areas, blackberry and raspberry vines cover trees, fences, and woodland, often growing in huge bushes the size of houses. They are easy to spot, and you can collect buckets full of the sweet berries in the late summer. (In the West, watch out for bears, who also like blackberries very much.) Blackberries are dark purple when ripe, while ripe raspberries are completely red. Thimbleberries are tart relatives of red raspberries that grow on thornless bushes in the western half of the United States and Canada. They are round and bright red when ripe. All three of these types of berries are aggregate berries (see p. 142). Remember: avoid picking fruit from plants that have single berries unless you are absolutely sure that what you are eating is safe.

- **Cattails.** Most wet places have cattails. The young stems (found in the early spring) can be eaten raw, but they are often better tasting when they've been boiled in water a few minutes. The flower heads, which are covered with pollen, can be eaten in the very early spring. When they turn into brown, smooth shapes that look sort of like fuzzy hot dogs, the tops are no longer good to eat. The roots of a cattail can be peeled and cooked in boiling water, but they taste pretty awful if they're from a cattail that has grown in muddy, dirty water. Overall, cattails that grow in deep, clear water are much better tasting. Keep in mind that if the plant is growing in dirty, polluted water, it needs to be cooked thoroughly before eating.

- **Red clover and wild grasses.** The stems, leaves, and flowers of clover can be eaten. The flowers can be used as tea. The good thing about clover is that often you will find entire fields of it. All grasses are good to chew on *except* those with purple, pink, or black seeds (grass seeds are usually green)—these might have a fungus that could kill you. If you can't tell the seed color, don't eat it.

- **Wild rose hips.** Wild roses grow in many places. They look a lot like the roses you might plant in your yard, but the flowers have a single row of petals, not the bunches of petals that you are used to seeing. Rose hips are the red seedpods that show up on the plants from summer to fall. Rose hips don't always have much taste, but they're full of vitamin C.

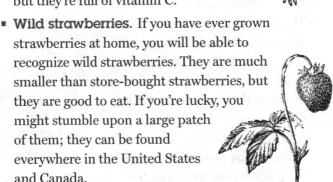

- **Wild strawberries.** If you have ever grown strawberries at home, you will be able to recognize wild strawberries. They are much smaller than store-bought strawberries, but they are good to eat. If you're lucky, you might stumble upon a large patch of them; they can be found everywhere in the United States and Canada.

- **Dandelions.** These small plants are found nearly everywhere, often growing in people's lawns. They can be recognized by their jagged leaves that grow directly out of the ground and by their yellow flowers, which start off dense and bright yellow but turn into white, wispy "puffballs" full of tiny seeds. There are a few plants that look similar, but they do not have the bright yellow flowers and their leaves grow out of a main center stalk instead of the ground. Very young dandelion leaves are good to eat raw; they taste like spinach. (In fact, my local market sells them mixed with other greens for salads.) Larger plants, which are older, can be bitter, and their leaves need to be boiled in water before they can be eaten. Dandelion leaves are full of minerals and vitamins.

- **Prickly pear and other cactus fruits.** These red or orange fruits that grow at the ends of some cactus pads are good to eat, but you have to peel them first. Some have to be put in the fire to cook off the little thorns that cover them before you peel them. The pads of the prickly pear cactus are also edible, but they must be cooked and the thorns must be scraped off first.

- **Mormon tea.** This bushy desert plant with no noticeable leaves has a chemical in it that makes you active and alert when you boil it in water to make a tea.

- **Seaweed.** Most types of seaweed are edible, tasty, and packed with vitamins and protein. Gather seaweed that is still growing in the ocean; don't

eat any that has been sitting on the beach. Although no variety of seaweed is poisonous, not every one is edible. Kelp, green seaweed, Irish moss, bladder wrack, and sea lettuce are most often eaten. Sea lettuce looks like bright green, leafy lettuce and is found all over the world. Irish moss is a common, small, reddish-brown bushy plant that attaches itself to rocks. Bull kelp is an enormous plant with feet of stems held up by round gas-filled bladders that grows along on the western coast of the United States and Canada. Cook the tough varieties like giant kelp in water or roast them over the fire. The small, tender varieties can be eaten raw or cooked. If you are unsure whether the water they grew in is polluted, do not eat them raw.

KELP

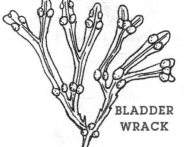

BLADDER WRACK

IRISH MOSS

Kids who spend lots of time outdoors often learn about local plants that are both safe to eat and tasty. For instance, many kids who live in western states from Colorado to the Pacific Ocean know that ripe manzanita berries taste like dried cranberries and are a delicious treat—but that knowledge would be of no help to someone who's living in Florida, where manzanitas don't grow. Kids who live in desert areas know all about prickly pear fruits and snack on mesquite beans when they go hiking, but have no idea what a huckleberry looks like. Children on the East Coast and in the Rocky Mountains see blueberries in the wild regularly, but their friends on the Kansas plains or the California coast may never come across a single one. Your local bookstore or library has books that can help you learn about edible wild plants that grow in your particular area, or you can check out the websites in the resources section (p. 207) for more information.

MANZANITA

ACTIVITY

FINDING WILD EDIBLES

Get your parents' permission before you do this activity. Get a book on edible plants that grow in your area from a library or bookstore. Using it as a reference, look around your neighborhood and see how many edible plants you can spot. You might be surprised to find many edible plants growing in vacant lots, city parks, or even your own backyard. Remember, though: *do not eat any plant, seed, or fruit unless you are 100 percent sure that it's safe to eat.*

EDIBLE ANIMALS

Many animals that you may you encounter in the wilderness can be killed, cooked, and eaten—but before you go hunting, consider the drawbacks. You will probably be rescued within a day or so, and your main job is to stay healthy and safe until then. You can put yourself in grave danger by trying to kill a rattlesnake, a scorpion, or a snapping turtle. Are you really that hungry?

If you do decide to hunt for food, the following animals are your best options:

- **Fish.** All fish you may encounter are edible. That doesn't mean that they all taste wonderful. Sucker fish and other bottom dwellers taste muddy. Trout, bass, salmon, and catfish taste much better. It couldn't hurt to carry some fishing line, hooks, and lures in your survival kit. If you go fishing often, you know that many times fish do not bite, no matter what you do, so having fishing equipment does not guarantee that you'll be able to enjoy a fish dinner, but it doesn't hurt to have them when you're in a survival situation. If you don't have fishing equipment, you might be able to catch fish with your hands in shallow water, or you can make a fish trap: Stick rocks or twigs into the bottom of a stream in the shape of a large V or U. If you're lucky, fish will swim down the stream, into the wide part of the V, and down into the small end of the V, where you can grab them. Make it easy for the fish to swim into your trap, but difficult to escape it. You can also use a plastic food bag to scoop up small fish in shallow water. Or if you have a plastic soda bottle, you can make another type of fish trap, for minnows: Cut off the small end of the plastic bottle about two inches below the top. Drop a few rocks and perhaps some bait into the now-open bottle. Put the cut bottle top back onto the bottle—but upside down so the mouth is facing into the bottle. Press it firmly into place. Put the trap into shallow water and let it fill up. Minnows can swim into the bottle but will not swim out; you can use them as bait to catch larger fish. Some kinds of fish carry diseases and parasites, so once you've caught one, you need to *gut* it. To do this, make a long cut along the belly of the fish, from the gills to the vent (the tiny opening near the tail). Using your fingers, pull out the guts and dispose of them away from your camp. Then cook the rest of the fish over the fire to kill the remaining germs. If you have clay soil around, you can wrap fish in a layer of clay and stick the whole thing in the fire. The clay will bake and cook the fish inside it. You can also drape the fish over a green, *nonpoisonous* branch to cook it, or put it on a hot, flat stone in the coals.

- **Birds**. All birds are good to eat. So are their eggs. Catching them is another matter (unless, of course, you have a gun). You may be able to throw a rock or stick at one to stun it before you grab it. Birds must be plucked (their feathers must be removed) or skinned, cleaned, and cooked well before they can be eaten. To clean a bird, first remove and discard the head. Then make a shallow cut all the way down the length of the bird's underside from the tail to the neck. Be careful not to cut into the internal organs— they are filled with bacteria. Open up the cavity with your hands, reach inside toward the spine, and pull out the stomach, intestine, and internal organs. Discard these. If you can, rinse the bird carcass in clean water. Cook the bird as soon as possible by roasting it on a stick over a fire. You can also collect bird eggs, boil them in water for a few minutes, and then eat them.

- **Frogs**. Remember to *leave toads and salamanders alone*. Many are poisonous. Frog legs, on the other hand, are good to eat. (Chapter 6, p. 101, explains how to tell the difference between toads and frogs, but if you're still not sure you can tell the difference, stay away from frogs too.) Kill the frogs, skin them, and cut off the hind legs. The legs need to be cooked over a fire or boiled.

- **Mussels, clams, and snails**. If you're in an area that's near water, you have many food sources that are not available inland. Mussels and clams are found in lots of bodies of water, and they taste great. As a general rule, do not eat mussels or clams collected from the ocean from May to November. During these warmer months, they can contain toxic algae and bacteria that make them very dangerous to eat. Freshwater mussels can be eaten year-round, but they must be cooked right after you pull them from the water, and you'll need to remove and discard the hairy "beard" on the outside of the shell. With both mussels and clams, clean the outside and throw out any that are not tightly closed or have unusually heavy shells—that's an indication that they are filled with sand. Steam the rest of them over coals or on a flat rock in the fire or cook them in a little water until they open. Small snails can also be boiled in water for nourishment. Cook them well. Only eat those with clear fluid inside. If you squeeze them and see green liquid, toss them.

- **Crayfish.** Crayfish, which are also known as crawdads and crawfish, are some of the best-tasting and easiest-to-find survival foods in areas that are near water. They look like miniature lobsters, and you can find them along the bottoms of streams and rivers all over the United States and Canada. Boil them whole in water or cook them over a fire, then eat the meat in the claws and tail.

- **Snakes.** Small nonvenomous snakes are good to eat but tough to prepare. You need to remove all the skin, cut the snake open lengthwise along its belly (being careful not to cut into the organs inside), and remove the guts in an intact mass without rupturing them. *Do not try to eat a venomous snake.* (See "Venomous Snakes," p. 91). Rattlesnakes, water moccasins, and the other venomous snakes are edible, but they're hard to kill and difficult to handle safely. The heads will bite you long after you have removed them.

- **Small mammals.** Squirrels, rabbits, rats, mice, and other small mammals are all edible, but these animals bite and are hard to catch. They must be trapped or shot, and then they have to be skinned, cleaned, and cooked thoroughly.

- **Insects.** Grasshoppers, maggots (fly larvae), large ants, and other insects are also edible. Grasshoppers, crickets, and maggots may have diseases and parasites, like tapeworms, that could make you sick if you eat them raw, so be sure to cook them well. Ants can be cooked, too, although they don't have to be. When eating large ants, don't eat the heads; they will bite your mouth or tongue. Several boys in my survival classes have told me that ants taste tart. I took their word for it.

You don't want to cut cooked meat with the same knife you used to prepare the meat when it was raw without sterilizing it first. After cutting open any raw meat or fish, sterilize your knife by sticking the blade into the fire or hot coals for one minute to kill anything that might make you sick.

10

LEARNING TO NAVIGATE

For some people, navigation or orienteering—finding your way with a map and compass or GPS—is an enjoyable and endlessly fascinating puzzle. Other people (like me) have paralyzing math anxiety just looking at a compass and a topographic map. I had to take orienteering classes repeatedly, to the annoyance of my teachers, before I figured out what I was doing. It can be frustrating to keep track of where you are and where you're going—unless you think about how this information could prevent you from getting lost or help you find your way again if you do. Let's start with the basics:

- The sun rises in the east and sets in the west. Don't forget it. You would be surprised to learn how many people don't know that. Sunrise comes before sunset, and "E" comes before "W" in the alphabet, so east and sunrise go together.

- A compass's directional needle always points to the north. That's how you use it to find your way. If you look at a compass, the directions, clockwise from the point of the needle, are north, then east, then south, and finally west. To remind yourself of the order— N, E, S, W—remember the saying "**N**ever **E**at **S**hredded **W**heat."

- The easiest way to find out where you are on a map is to hold the map in front of you and then look at the wilderness around you for landmarks. Is there a tall mountain? A lake? A road? Try to match any landmarks you find to their representations on the map. If you see a lake to your west and a tall skinny peak to your north, and then you find the same two things on the map, you are on your way to figuring out where you are. Now turn the map so that it mirrors the scenery; this is called *orienting the map*.

What good does all this information do you? If you have a compass and you know what direction you walked in before you got lost, you can reverse direction and find your way back to familiar ground. If you also have a map, you can figure out where you are, how you got there, and how to get home.

Let's look at an example. Say that you are in a campground just south of a large lake. One afternoon you decide to go fishing with your younger brother—without navigation equipment. There is a trail that circles the entire lake. Both of you walk north around the west (left) side of the lake for about a mile and find a fishing spot. After fishing for a few hours, you head back to camp in the late afternoon—but because you don't have a compass, you accidentally head north instead of south. You end up walking all around the north end of the lake, away from camp. You find yourself still walking as night falls. Now it's pitch dark and you have no idea where you are or why you have not found your camp. If you'd had a compass, you could have checked it as you were walking to the lake and seen that you were headed north. Then, when you were ready to come back to camp, you could have checked your compass again to make sure that you were walking in the opposite direction—south.

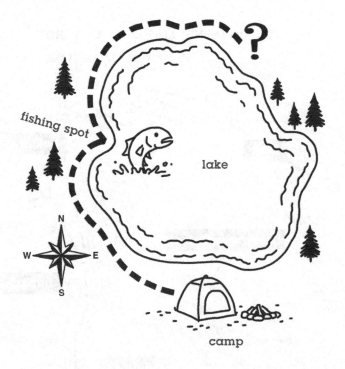

CHOOSING A MAP

All maps are helpful for finding your way, but some types are better for explorers in the outdoors. A *topographic map*, or *topo map*, shows the mountains and hills in an area as brown, wavy lines. The closer the lines, the steeper the hill or mountain. Every fifth line usually shows the elevation in feet. With some practice, you can match the outlines on the topographic map to the landmarks you see around you. Topographic maps are always laid out with north at the top.

TOPOGRAPHIC MAP OF LAKE TAHOE

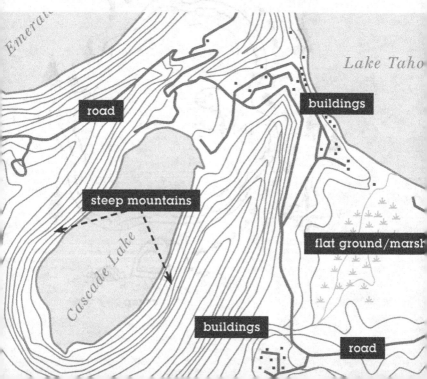

What you see

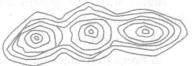

What it looks like on a topographical map

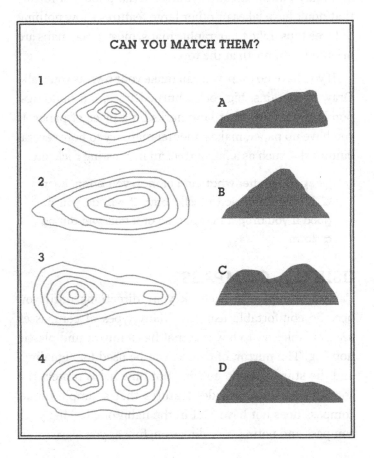

CAN YOU MATCH THEM?

1

A

2

B

3

C

4

D

Aerial maps are actually photographs; they show the land as you might see it from an airplane. These maps, which are widely available on the Internet, are very helpful in areas that don't have heavy forest: you can see all the trails, lakes, rivers, buildings, mountains, and other landmarks in the area. Of course, aerial photos of forests that don't have lakes or other large features show nothing but tree tops. Like topographic maps, most aerial maps are oriented with north at the top.

If you have no map, you can make your own as you walk. Draw mountains, big rocks, burned trees, old buildings, ponds, fences, or other landmarks on a piece of paper. If you have no paper, make a mental map: try to note several landmarks, such as a fallen tree, an interesting rock, etc.

> ☒ **No matter what kind of map you bring, keep it in a sealed plastic bag. It will do you no good if you drop it in a puddle or it gets wet during a storm.**

USING A COMPASS

Carry a compass and check your directions until you become comfortable using it. Many types of compasses are available; try to buy one that has a mirror and plastic housing. The mirror, of course, can be used for signaling, and the sturdy plastic housing not only helps protect the compass but also provides features that a simple round compass does not have. Get in the habit of checking your compass and noting your direction, first as you leave camp to explore, and then periodically afterward as you walk to keep on track. When you're out adventuring, tell yourself or whoever is with you, "I left north and walked along a straight path for half an hour, then turned northeast and walked for another half hour." When it is time to go back, what direction would you go? You would walk southwest for about half an hour, and then go south for another half hour.

So how do you read your compass? Let's look at the parts of a compass first. The most important part, of course, is the *directional needle*. No matter which way you turn, the needle will point north. The needle is usually colored red at one end and black or white at the other end. The red end is the part that points north.

You may think that a compass that's pointing north is pointing directly toward the North Pole, but that isn't true. Compasses point toward a constantly shifting point some distance away called the *magnetic North Pole*. In many places, the distance between the two poles—known as their *declination*—is so great that a compass needs to be adjusted, usually by moving a screw or twisting a ring, so that it gives you a more accurate reading. For instance, while the declination is 0 degrees in Iowa, it is 14 degrees in California and –16 degrees in Maine. Most compasses come with instructions on how to adjust them, and most topographic maps have a *declination number* in the lower left corner to indicate the proper adjustment for the area.

Of course, you need to know how to use your compass to find directions other than north. Suppose you don't have a map but you remember that there is a road northwest of you. If you can just figure out where northwest is, you can hit the road. How do you use a compass to find northwest? That's what the other compass parts are for.

While each model is different, your compass should look something like the one in the illustration below. See the ring around the needle? That's the *compass housing*, and it turns. It has little notches on it called *degrees*. There are 360 degrees. At one end of the compass is an arrow. That is your direction of travel arrow. Suppose you want to walk northwest, which is halfway between north and west; turn the housing ring so that the *direction of travel arrow* is set to the spot midway between north and west.

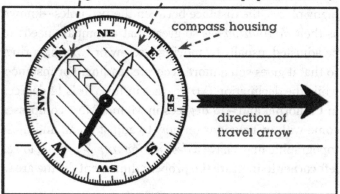

PARTS OF COMPASS
orienting arrow

directional needle
(red end always points north)

compass housing

direction of
travel arrow

Now hold the compass flat in your hand and turn your body around until you see that the red end of the directional needle has lined up within the *orienting arrow* below it. Usually the solid red directional needle will be lined up inside the larger, open orienting arrow. The needle and the orienting arrow should *both* be pointing north. Ask yourself, "Is the red in the shed?" That means, "Are the red needle and the orienting arrow both pointing north?" Double check to make sure that it's the red end of the needle, not the opposite (black or white) end that is pointing north—if you don't get this part right, you will go in the opposite direction from where you intended!

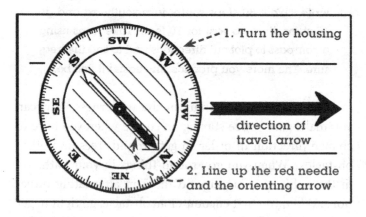

1. Turn the housing

direction of travel arrow

2. Line up the red needle and the orienting arrow

Look again at your direction of travel arrow. It should now be pointing to the northwest. Face that direction. What do you see northwest of you? Is there a landmark? Perhaps a big rock? Or does northwest fall in a space between two tall trees that you can use as a mental landmark? Head for whatever northwest landmark you can find. When you reach it, stop and find northwest again from there; this is called *taking a bearing*.

You now know how to use a compass. If you want further instructions and suggestions on perfecting your skills, check your local library or bookstore for books on navigation and orienteering or visit the orienteering websites listed in the resources section (p. 207).

ACTIVITY The best way to practice using a compass is to hide something and write out directions so a friend can find it. For example, you might write, "Walk 30 steps south, turn southeast and go 15 steps, then go east for 10 feet." Take turns using a compass to plot out directions and to find the treasure. The more you practice, the easier it will be.

When you're out walking in the wilderness, how can you make sure you're staying on course when you have to change direction in order to get around trees and other obstacles? When you go around things in your path, get in the habit of going around them in alternating directions. When you first encounter an obstacle, go right to get around it. To get around the next obstacle, go left. This helps to keep you moving in a fairly straight path. Weirdly enough, most people who become lost end up drifting in a clockwise direction. Don't let that happen to you!

To make sure that your compass works properly, keep it away from your GPS, cell phone, or any metal object, because their magnetic fields can draw the compass needle in the wrong direction. In addition, there is a liquid inside the housing that allows your needle to float, and extreme conditions can cause the liquid to leak. So do not get insect repellent on it or leave it in the hot sun—and, of course, try not to drop it.

OTHER WAYS TO ORIENT YOURSELF

What do you do if you don't have a compass with you? *Do not* try to determine your direction based on the old belief that moss only grows on the north side of a rock or a tree. It is true that there are usually fewer branches on the north side of a tree and that moss sometimes grows more thickly on that side. However, moss often grows on *all* sides of rocks and trees, especially in damp or thick forests.

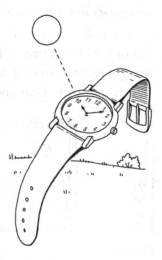

Fortunately, there are several other ways to tell directions. First, you can use your watch. Hold it face up and flat so that it's level with the ground and line up the hour hand with the sun. Next, imagine a line halfway between the hour hand and the 12. That is your north-south line—the part of the line in front of you is pointing south.

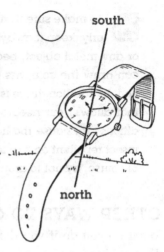

What if you don't have a watch, or your watch is digital or on your cell phone? If you know what time it is—say, three in the afternoon—you can draw a clock in the dirt with the hour hand at the current hour aiming at the sun. Then imagine that there's a line halfway between the hour hand and where the 12 would be. The front part of that imaginary line also points south.

If you don't know the time, you can make a compass out of a stick and two rocks. In an open spot, push a stick upright into the ground. Mark where the top of its shadow falls with a rock. Wait about 30 minutes, and then mark

STEP 1

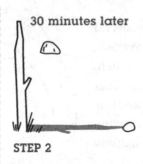

30 minutes later

STEP 2

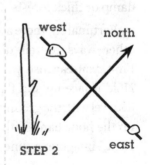

west   north

east

STEP 2

the next shadow's top with another rock. Stand with your left foot at your first rock and your right foot at the second rock. You are now facing north.

If it's nighttime, you won't be able to use a stick or your watch to make a compass. But you can navigate by the stars instead. Although it seems like the stars move across the sky, the North Star, also known as the polestar, stays basically in one spot, so you can use it to figure out which way is north. The North Star is not the biggest or brightest star in the sky, but it is fairly easy to find. Just look for the Little and Big Dippers. Locate the two stars that make up the outside edge of the Big Dipper's cup. Imagine drawing a straight line through those two stars toward the Little Dipper's handle. That line points to the North Star, which is the last star in the Little Dipper's handle. After you find the

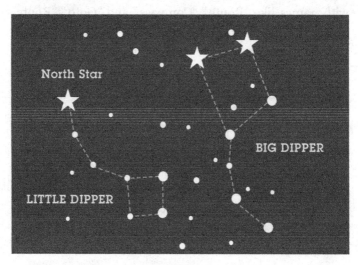

North Star in the night sky, place a stick pointing toward it with a rock at one end to mark the north end. *In the morning*, when you can safely see where you are walking, you will know which direction to go. Walking at night is dangerous; in the dark, you cannot see hazards and you run a big risk of injury. Stay safe and wait until morning to head out.

GPS

GPS stands for Global Positioning System. It's an electronic device that figures out your location by tracking you with satellites. There are many types: Some are used in cars and others are carried by hikers. Some are very expensive and have many features; others are less pricey and have only a few essential functions. Most GPS units have functions with names like "Route," "Compass," and "Goto." "Route" (or "Map") shows you on a map where you have walked, and "Goto" shows you the path you need to take to get to a certain point, and "Compass" displays a digital compass.

Every GPS reports your location as a set of numbers, but these numbers may be displayed either as standard latitude and longitude numbers or as UTM numbers. In the UTM (Universal Transverse Mercator) system, the globe is "flattened" and divided into 60 regions; your location is translated into Eastings and Northings numbers instead of latitude and longitude numbers. When first setting up their GPS devices, most Americans pick the UTM setting of "NAD 27 CONUS." That stands for "North American datum, continental United States." Why do you need to know about these different kinds of coordinate systems? If you share location information with someone else, like the people searching for you, you need to make sure they know what coordinate system you're using.

For example, suppose you have cell phone coverage and you are able to call emergency services. They ask you if you have a GPS and request your location coordinates. You read off your coordinates in UTM, NAD 27 CONUS mode, but the searchers assume you are using latitude and longitude. They may end up searching for you many miles from your location.

Your GPS screen will have a map that shows where you are, as well as a digital compass page. On the compass page, a big arrow shows you which direction you are heading, and the rotating ring moves around automatically to find north. You can use either the map or the compass page to find your way back home. If you marked your starting point, called a waypoint, by pressing the "Mark" key, you will be able to see your path from start to finish on the map page. To find your way back, you just set your GPS to go to your starting point and follow the path shown on the screen or the pointing arrow on your compass page.

Every company makes different models of GPS units, each with its own features and complexity. Start with a simple model and learn how to use it. Like so many other things in life, it takes practice to learn how to use one, but once you've mastered it the GPS can be wonderfully helpful.

ACTIVITY

GEOCACHING

You and your friends can go *geocaching* to learn how use a GPS. This is a treasure hunt that uses GPS units. All over the world, adventurers like you have hidden more than a million containers called *geocaches* in outdoor locations. They post the geocaches' GPS coordinates on the Internet, and other people use their GPS units to find them and see what is hidden inside. The container may be a plastic food container, an ammo box, or a bucket. Most geocaches contain a logbook for you to record your name and the date; many contain a number of items to trade. If you take an item out of a geocache, leave something else in return—something good. Now that geocaching has become popular, more and more people take the cool trade items and leave junk. The item you add doesn't have to be expensive, but leave the fast food toy prizes at home and pick up some fun items at your local dollar store to leave. To find a geocache in your area, visit a geocaching website such as www.geocaching.com.

Be careful when reaching for a geocache. Geocachers often hide their containers in holes so that they are harder to find and less likely to be noticed by casual hikers in the area. But other things can end up hiding in those holes along with the geocaches. A woman in my area was bitten by a rattlesnake while reaching into a geocaching hole.

GPS units are great. I have three of them, and I love them all. However, some models have trouble communicating with their satellites if you are under heavy tree cover or down in a canyon. Your path on the map screen might have a few bits missing if you walk through these areas. GPS units also lose power pretty quickly; you need to always carry spare batteries. And remember: don't put your compass and GPS together or near each other. Each one interferes with the other.

11

WHAT TO DO IF YOU OR SOMEONE ELSE IS INJURED

If your brother or sister suffered a bad fall when there were no adults around, would you know what to do? Suppose you were hiking with your best friend and he was bitten by a rattlesnake. What would you do? What if you yourself got frostbite, or a burn from a campfire? Would you be prepared? These are all situations in which knowledge of first aid can be a lifesaver. First aid involves using common sense and basic knowledge to take care of yourself and others.

This book provides very basic information on first aid. It is no substitute for taking a good first-aid class that gives you hands-on instructions on performing CPR, bandaging arms and legs, treating wounds, and many other activities. Check to see if your school, your local Red Cross office, or your local Girl Scouts or Boy Scouts offer first-aid classes.

Previous chapters have already discussed how to handle snakebites (p. 97), bug bites and stings (p. 107), exposure to poison ivy, poison oak, and poison sumac (p. 143), and weather-related conditions such as hypothermia (p. 125) and frostbite (p. 131). In this chapter, you'll learn more general first-aid guidelines, and you'll find out how to treat physical injuries such as cuts, burns, and broken bones.

SAFETY FIRST

Once I stopped to help a person whose car had crashed. I immediately began to administer first aid, completely forgetting to do my most important job first: I did not check to make sure the area was safe. The victim, who was still behind the wheel of her car, started to pass out. Her car rolled forward and almost ran over three firemen! Before helping anyone, you must always make sure you and others are safe. Are you in a road where a car could hit you? Are there bees swarming around you? Do you need to move yourself and the person you're helping to safety?

❌ **Never** move people who are badly injured or unconscious unless it is too dangerous to leave them where they are—for instance, if they're in a burning car or in cold water. If you move people who have neck and back injuries, you can cause damage and leave them paralyzed.

As soon as you're sure that you and the injured person are safe, call the person's name and tap her gently. If she responds, ask her what happened and where it hurts. If there is no response, she might be unconscious. If so, your next step is to check her breathing. Watch her chest to see if it moves up and down, or put your ear next to her face. You can feel and listen for air coming out of her mouth. If she is not breathing, you need to make sure that her airway is open and then start CPR. The best way to learn CPR is to take a class on it and practice on a mannequin. There are different CPR methods for infants, children, and adults. Some sources now recommend no rescue breathing and only chest compressions for adults.

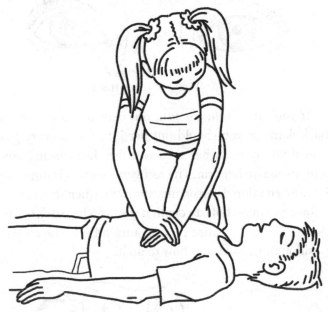

If the person is breathing but you cannot wake him up, try to determine whether he has any neck or back damage. Sometimes you can tell that a person has a severe head or neck injury by looking at his eyes—one pupil (the black part) might be bigger than another. Consider what you know about the person's injury as well: if he fell from somewhere high, it's quite possible that he injured his neck or back, but if he just collapsed to the ground where he was standing, he probably didn't.

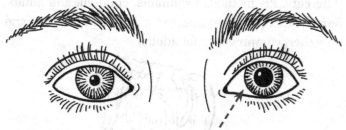

one pupil larger than the other

If you are *absolutely sure* the person has no neck or back damage, you should put her into the *recovery position* if you can: on her side, with her head facing down and resting on her arm. The recovery position is important because an injured person may throw up when she is unconscious. She may choke to death if she is on her back or facedown. You can practice putting a friend into the recovery position until you know how to do it.

RECOVERY POSITION

You can also take a pulse of someone who is sick or injured in order to help determine the person's condition. Pulses are found on the wrist and in the front area of the neck. A strong and steady pulse is a good sign. A very weak but fast pulse is a sign that the person may be going into shock. You can practice taking a pulse on yourself so you'll know where to find one if you need to help someone else.

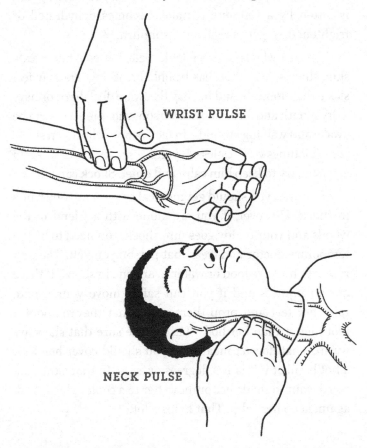

WRIST PULSE

NECK PULSE

SHOCK

What is shock? It's a dangerous medical condition that occurs when body organs and tissue don't get the right amount of blood flowing to them. Low blood flow means less oxygen to your brain, heart, and other vital organs. Shock can happen when a person is injured, sick, or cold. It can also happen when a person eats a poisonous plant, is bitten by a venomous snake, becomes dehydrated or frightened, or gets a really bad sunburn.

A person who is in shock looks pale, has cool but sweaty skin, shivers, and often has trouble breathing. He may feel sick to his stomach, and he may throw up, feel dizzy, or have a dry mouth and feel thirsty. A person who is in shock can be awake and walking around—in fact, people who are in shock are sometimes very restless. If you see symptoms of shock in a person, try to keep him calm and quiet. Shock can kill.

Of course, you should get medical care for anyone who's in shock. However, if you are alone with a friend in the woods and your buddy goes into shock, you need to be the temporary doctor and treat that person yourself. The first rule is to not give food or water to anyone in shock. If there are no injuries and if you can safely move your friend, raise her feet and prop them up so that they're about a foot higher than her body. Last, make sure that she stays warm. That doesn't mean that you should cover her with a hot blanket if it is 110 degrees outside. In that situation, you'd want to shade her or move her to a cooler place. And, again, keep her calm. That helps a lot.

CUTS

When you are treating someone who has a cut or you are dealing with a cut on your own body, wear plastic or latex gloves if you can. If you don't have any, put a clean plastic bag over each hand to help keep germs from your hands out of the cut. It's great if you can also wash your hands with warm water and plenty of soap beforehand, but there aren't many sinks and soap dispensers in the wilderness.

If the cut is bleeding badly, press hard on the wound with your gloved or bagged hand for a few minutes. Then, if you have a clean pad of paper towels, tissues, or cloth, quickly take your hand away, cover the wound with the pad, and press hard. If you don't have any of these things handy, just keep your hand over the wound. You don't want someone to gush blood while you are looking all over for a clean bandage and gloves.

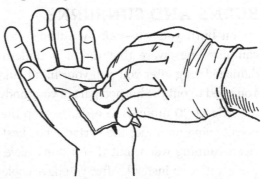

Try to lift the bleeding part of the body up to slow down the bleeding, but only if it does not hurt to move it. If there is a broken bone, you don't want to move anything. If there is still blood coming through, place another pad on top of the first one. Press down on it until the bleeding stops. If you have tape, use it to tape all of the pads in place after the bleeding has stopped.

To treat a small cut, rinse the wound with clean water if you have any. If you have soap, use that as well. Try to make sure that no dirt stays in the cut. Put an antiseptic from your first-aid kit on the wound (see chapter 12, p. 202) and cover it with a clean bandage.

Remember, if someone has been hurt, one of the best things you can do is to try to keep him calm. Injured people feel better knowing what is happening, so tell him what treatment you are doing. And try not to panic yourself. Your friend is counting on you for help, so please don't freak out.

BURNS AND SUNBURNS

If you burn yourself—say, by putting your hand in the campfire—be aware that the skin underneath is being damaged long after you pull your hand out of the flames. You need to put the burned part of your body in cold water for at least 20 minutes in order to stop the burning that is still going on under the surface. The best thing is cold, clean running water, but if you don't have that, you can use a wet cloth instead. After you have cooled off the area, cover it with a clean, loose bandage. If blisters form, *do not* break them. If they break on their own, use antibiotic ointment on the open areas. *Do not* use butter or oil on a burn. It will keep it from healing. You may want to take pain-relief tablets, though—see chapter 12 (p. 203) for information on how to stock your first-aid kit.

The same techniques you use to treat burns should be used to treat sunburns: cool the burned skin with water, try not to break blisters, and use antibiotic ointment and, if necessary, pain-relief medication. You can use aloe vera lotion to sooth skin that is mildly sunburned.

BROKEN BONES AND SPRAINS

Your bones are actually living things, and if they break they will bleed into the tissue around them. Large bones leak more blood than small ones, and your body will swell around the break. Broken bones hurt and can make people feel sick and scared. Kids can even go into shock from a broken bone. Sprains, too, can be very painful. A *sprain* is an injury to the muscles, ligaments, and tendons around a joint such as your ankle. You can't always tell the difference between a broken bone and a sprain, so the two should be treated in the same way.

What do you do with a body part that may be sprained or broken? Broken bones hurt a lot, so do not touch the injured area. If you are far from help, there are still some things you can do to make the injured person more comfortable. You can create a *splint* to keep the injured part of the body from moving and causing more pain and damage. To make a splint, find something that will hold the injured part in place: several sticks, part of a backpack, a rolled-up newspaper, pieces of cardboard, or anything else that's firm should work. (Once, when I was on a camping trip, I splinted a friend's broken arm with two sticks wrapped in newspaper and some duct tape. It worked so well that the arm hardly swelled at all during the long ride to the hospital.) Lay splints on *both* sides of the injured area to brace it, making sure that the splints extend both above and below the injury. Then gently tape or tie your splint to the injured limb.

If you have ice or a cool cloth, gently put it on the broken part to keep the swelling down. This will also help with the pain. Don't put ice directly on the injury; wrap it in something first, like a bandanna. Pain-relief tablets may help the injured person to feel a bit more comfortable, too.

To hold an injured arm or wrist in place, you can make a *sling* instead of a splint. Use a shirt or tear off a piece of tarp. A sling needs to be comfortable when tied around the neck.

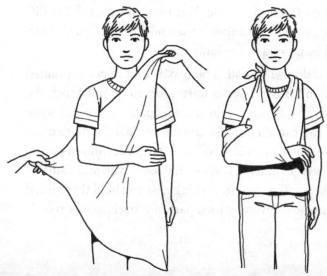

What if you hurt your ankle? If you have cold water, put your hurt foot in cold water for a while to help keep the swelling down, then splint it. There are lots of ways to make an ankle splint. For instance, you could use your shoe or hiking boot, then tie a sling or a bandanna under the heel and firmly around the ankle to keep the foot from moving around. Duct tape could be in the same way, over your boot or even just over your sock. What else could you use? How about a shirt sleeve? Or if you have an elastic bandage, wrap it around, above, around, and below the ankle to stabilize it and keep it from twisting. You want your splint to hold the foot steady, but not so tightly that it cuts off circulation.

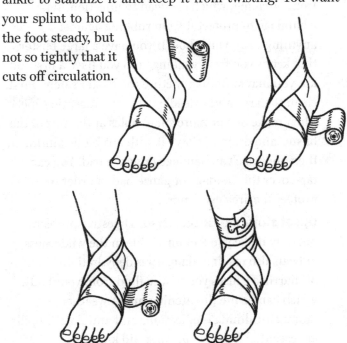

It's very common for people to break a finger. I have broken almost every one of mine over the years. It's easy to make a splint for an injured finger—just tape it to the fingers that are next to it, or tape it to a small stick.

OTHER MEDICAL ISSUES

Out in the wilderness, you may also encounter the following medical issues:

- **Blisters**. Everyone gets blisters, especially hikers. They can be very painful. Try to keep the blister from breaking, which can lead to infection. Wrap it in a bandage to protect it from rubbing against anything—say, your shoe. If you have a large blister that keeps you from walking, and you have a first-aid kit, you may want to puncture the blister safely: First, clean the area and a needle with an antiseptic wipe. Then make one or more small holes at the side of the blister and drain it. Cover it with antibiotic ointment, then apply a clean bandage or gauze pad. You can tape over the bandage or gauze pad in order to protect the area even more.

- **Upset stomach or diarrhea**. Digestive problems not only make you feel miserable in the wilderness but can also result in dangerous dehydration. Vomiting or diarrhea causes you to lose fluid from your body, which can be life threatening in hot weather. Stomach-calming medications and antidiarrhea pills are essential items in any first-aid kit.

- **Nosebleeds.** If you have a nosebleed, sit and lean forward so that you're looking down at the ground. Pinch the sides of your nose at the soft part and hold it for 10 minutes.

- **Splinters.** Splinters often cause infection and should be removed if possible. Use tweezers to pull the end of the splinter out of the skin—be sure to pull in the same direction that the splinter went in. Disinfect or wash the area where the splinter was removed. If the splinter is underneath the skin, use a needle or safety pin that you have cleaned with an antiseptic wipe to move the splinter until you can grab it with tweezers and pull it out.

- **Drugs and alcohol.** Drugs and alcohol can be deadly if you are in bad weather or lost in the wild. I know of several instances in which healthy young people died in survival situations because they were high on drugs and they panicked when their lives were in danger. Because of the drugs, the kids were unable to evaluate their situation, make survival plans, or think clearly. They died of hypothermia within a few hours of becoming lost. They would have survived if their minds had been sharp instead of confused and clouded by drugs.

12

PACKING A
SURVIVAL KIT

Throughout this book, you've read about the items you need
to bring with you to build a shelter, start a fire, or face other
survival challenges. This chapter provides a quick reference
to *all* the items you should carry on any hike or adventuring
trip in the wilderness—and why you need them. Many of
these items are inexpensive and easy to find. For instance,
one of the most useful survival tools is a plastic trash bag.

BASIC SURVIVAL KIT

Your basic survival kit should be small enough that you can
always have it with you. It doesn't help you much if it's left
in a car or closet, right? Your kit should include the following essential items, most of which are small and lightweight
enough to fit in a gallon-size plastic bag:

- **Toilet paper.** This should be at the top of your
  essential equipment list. In addition to its regular use,
  it makes pretty good fire-starting material.

- **Trash bags.** Big plastic trash bags can be used to line
  your shelter, make a blanket of leaves or mattress

of pine needles, or cover the top of your snow
trench. You can tear holes in the top and sides of one
to make a raincoat, or wave one to signal rescuers.
The best trash bags to bring are the extra-thick ones
called *contractor* bags, although orange-colored bags
are great for signaling. Sporting goods stores sell
orange trash bags, and you can buy contractor bags at
your local home improvement store. Carry at least two.

- **Whistle or air horn.** A loud whistle is really essential
  for signaling over a long distance. I like Storm
  whistles. They last forever and are super loud. An
  air horn is also handy for signaling. Most run on
  compressed air and will give you a hundred or
  more blasts.

- **Swiss Army–type knife or other multi-tool.**
  Another essential—get a good-quality one. With luck,
  you will only have to buy one or two in your lifetime.
  Learn how to sharpen the knife and keep it ready to
  use. Make sure you get one that has a saw blade.

- **Fire-starters, fire-starting materials, and tinder.**
  Fire-starting materials can be things as simple as
  toilet paper squares covered in melted wax or cotton
  balls dipped in petroleum jelly or as fancy as fire
  paste or a magnesium block. See chapter 5 (p. 62)
  for more information on your options. As for fire-
  starters, you can buy waterproof matches that ignite
  even when wet, and disposable lighters are cheap and
  dependable. You should carry both. You may also

want to carry your own tinder: steel wool, shredded paper, waxed paper, or fatwood sticks. You can keep your fire-building equipment in a little waterproof container or sealed plastic bag.

- **Nonperishable food.** Food gives you energy, improves your mood, and keeps you alert. Select high-calorie, nonperishable foods. Dehydrated meals are lightweight and easy to prepare as long as you are able to boil water; they're sold at many outdoor supply stores. MREs (meals ready to eat) are also great choices; they're sold at military supply stores and online. You can also carry sealed bags of jerky, peanuts, trail mix, nutrition bars, or candy bars with peanuts. Special survival bars that give you an entire day's supply of calories in one bar are sold at many sporting goods and outdoor supply stores.

- **Flashlight or headlamp and chemical light sticks.** A small flashlight or headlamp is another essential. Headlamps are especially useful, because you can carry materials for a shelter, get wood, and perform other activities without holding a flashlight in your hand. Always carry an extra set of batteries for your light. You should also carry several chemical light sticks in addition to a flashlight or a headlamp. They are inexpensive and handy to have to light your shelter or camp. Bend them and shake them, then hang them up.

- **Water purification tablets**. These come in basically two types, iodine or chlorine. To produce clean water, either type is added to a 32-ounce bottle of water, which is then stirred or shaken and left to sit according to package directions. The iodine tablets are especially effective but have an unpleasant aftertaste; after the water is purified, you can add vitamin C powder or other additives to improve the flavor. Both kinds of tablets are available at most sporting goods and outdoor supply stores. They should be replaced every year, or a week or so after the bottle has been opened (whichever comes first). If the tablets change color, throw them out.

- **Candle**. Everyone should carry at least one small candle. Candles can heat up a snow shelter, provide light, and help to light a fire.

- **Bandanna**. A bandanna has many uses. It can protect your head from the sun or your mouth from dust, filter your water, or splint a sprained ankle. Carry at least one.

- **Rope or cord**. This will help make a shelter or hang your food up away from bears. You can find sturdy *paracord* (known as paracord 550 or parachute cord) at sporting goods, hardware, and outdoor supply stores. It is unbelieveably strong and light. If you don't have cord, remember that you are wearing shoelaces.

- **Tarp or emergency blanket**. Look for a Mylar-lined tarp, also known as a space blanket; it's lightweight and far superior to a regular tarp when it comes to keeping you warm or protecting you from the heat. You can also buy small emergency blankets that fit in the palm of your hand—or, for real comfort, buy a bivvy sack made from the same material. These sacks weigh next to nothing and can be used as a sleeping bag. I have a double-size one, and both my dog and I snuggle inside it together. If you are facing cold weather, carry at least two tarps. You can line your shelter with one and wrap the other around you. Sporting goods stores and outdoor supply stores sell all kinds of tarps and blankets for use in the wilderness.

- **Water bottles**. Always carry at least two plastic 32-ounce water bottles—full of water, of course. If you need to collect more water later, you need the 32-ounce size for your purifying tablets. Be sure to use a recently manufactured bottle that is free of a potentially harmful compound called BPA.

- **Metal cup**. Metal camping cups are made for both drinking and cooking. You can boil water in them. Most have handles that fold down or come off. They are lightweight and they can fit easily into your day pack. They are sold at sporting goods and outdoor supply stores.

- **Compass and topographic map**. When selecting a compass, choose one that has plastic housing and a mirror. Be sure you know how to use it before you find yourself lost in the wilderness. And a compass is no good without a map of the area. Remember to protect your map from dirt and weather.

- **Signal mirror.** If you do not understand the compass, at least carry a small mirror for signaling. The light that's reflected by a signal mirror can easily be seen for over 10 miles, and up to 50 miles in the right conditions. Practice using your signal mirror before you head into the wilderness. Signal mirrors are available at many sporting goods and outdoor supply stores.

- **Plastic storage bags.** Plastic storage bags have so many uses: You can carry water in them or keep your fire-starting materials dry. They can protect your GPS and maps from rain. You can catch small fish in them, put them over your socks and under your shoes to keep your feet dry, or use them to melt snow in the sun or create a solar still. You can make waterproof mittens with the small ones, and the larger ones can hold all your survival gear or make a waterproof hat. Carry at least two sandwich-size and two gallon-size sealable plastic bags, as well as some twist ties to use to secure the bags to other things, such as branches to create a solar still (see p. 47).

- **Extra pair of socks.** A spare pair of socks can be a lifesaver if you get your feet wet. They weigh very

little, and they have many other uses as well: you
can use them to carry heated rocks or as mittens for
cold hands.

- **Cell phone or GPS.** Do you have a cell phone? Make
sure your GPS feature is activated. It might signal
where you are, even if you can't call out. In addition,
more and more kids have GPS devices. If you are
lucky enough to have a GPS for hiking, practice with
it often, and be sure to bring extra batteries.

- **Duct tape.** This silvery and strong tape can join
two tarps together, fix a shoe or torn parka, tape a
tarp to a rock, insulate a handle for a hot cup, and
splint an injured ankle. Sold at hardware stores, duct
tape is available in small rolls that are just perfect
for hikers.

- **Safety pins.** These take up almost no space but can
come in handy. You can pin a tarp and make a door
for your shelter, or make a sling. Bring four or five
of them.

- **First-aid kit.** Your survival kit should always include
a first-aid kit for emergencies. The next section will
explain what it should contain.

- **Insect repellent and mosquito netting.** Carry
insect repellent that is formulated to kill and repel
mosquitoes, ticks, and other bugs. Repellents that
contain *permethrin*—which is made from crushed
chrysanthemum flowers—are designed to be sprayed

only on clothing; they will last several days or so. Repellents that contain DEET, on the other hand, are made to be used on your skin; these sprays will last only a few hours. Many doctors recommend that kids use a low DEET formula (no more than 20 percent) which lasts between two and four hours. Finally, oil of lemon eucalyptus is a safe natural repellent that has been proven to work as well as DEET and lasts two hours. It is not recommended for kids under the age of three. Mosquito netting can help keep all kinds of biting insects off your head and face.

- **Hat, sunglasses, and gloves.** In cold weather, a winter hat is essential for protecting you from frostbite and hypothermia. Wool or fleece will hold in your body heat and protect your head and ears from the cold. In warm weather, a lightweight cowboy hat or wide-brimmed military-type hat will shade your head and eyes and help prevent heat illnesses. Sunglasses stop UV damage to your eyes in both summer and winter and protect your eyes from unseen low branches or blowing dust. Goggles or sunglasses can also save your eyes from injury while you're bushwhacking through the woods; late in the afternoon or in stormy weather, you do not always see sharp branches aimed toward your eyes. My neighbor Nick, who is a wild-land fire fighter, had his eye punctured by a sharp branch while working at dusk. Many firefighters and SAR team members now wear goggles when working in the deep woods. Finally, a pair of gloves will protect your hands from insect bites while gathering firewood, allow you to grab a hot cup, and keep your fingers warm.

The next group of items are not as essential as the previous, but they are also useful—and small enough to add to your pack without taking up much more space.

- **Paper and pen.** A notepad and a waterproof pen are good things to carry. If you want to signal to people looking for you, you can leave a note on the trail. If it is raining, you can put it in a plastic bag and put some rocks on top of it. You can also use the paper as a fire-starting material. I like Sharpie pens.

- **Flagging tape.** Bright-colored flagging tape is a great tool for signaling or marking your trail. Flagging tape is sold at outdoor supply stores and some sporting goods stores.

- **Vitamin C packets or sugared, flavored gelatin.** These can be added to water to take away the taste of iodine purification tablets, or just to give you an energy boost. Not only can sugary flavored gelatin be eaten, but brightly colored flavors can also be sprinkled on snow to signal rescuers.

- **Coffee filters.** Coffee filters weigh very little, and they can be used to filter (but not purify) water or as fire-starting material.

- **Disposable heat packs.** Chemically activated heat packs are awesome when you are in freezing conditions. Carry four or five of them and replace them every six months. It helps to have a few more than you'll need; I found that several did not work when I needed them, while others were still good after several years. The small ones are great in your shoes and gloves, and the ones with sticky backing can be affixed to whatever part of your body needs heat, such as your feet or under your arms. Heat packs of all sizes are sold at outdoor supply stores and some sporting goods stores.

- **Tube tent.** A single-person tube tent is another great thing to carry. Tube tents are tent-size plastic tubes with rope. You use the rope to attach the top of the tent to a tree or bush and close off the other end. Presto! You have a waterproof tent that you can use by itself, or you can build a brush shelter over it (see chapter 2, p. 29). Best yet, these tents take up little room in your pack. They are available at outdoor supply stores.

- **Watch.** A watch will tell you how long you have been gone, how long until sunrise during a long night, and most important, how to find directions if you have no compass (see chapter 10, p. 169). Select a watch that's waterproof or water resistant. Outdoor supply stores carry watches that come with compasses built right into them.

- **Fishing line, hooks, and lures.** You can wind fishing line around a small piece of folded cardboard and tuck in some hooks and a small lure or two.

- **Bear spray and bear bells.** Pepper spray made just for repelling bears, mountain lions, and other dangerous animals is recommended in many parks and forests. It is specially made to spray a long distance to deter attacks. *Do not* buy small spray dispensers made for defense against humans; they are not able to do the job. Bear spray is widely available in outdoor supply stores and online. Outdoor supply stores also sell bear bells, little bells with a Velcro strap that allows you to attach them to dog collars and packs. They give bears warning that you are in the area.

BASIC FIRST-AID KIT

A first-aid kit is important for dealing with the common injuries you or your friends might face in the wilderness until you can get to a doctor. Most of these supplies can be found at your local drugstore.

- **Disposable gloves.** Wear gloves when touching wounds, burns, or bodily fluids. It keeps you from getting any diseases and helps prevent infection of the wound or burn.

- **Tissues or gauze pads.** These are essential for cleaning wounds before using antiseptic wipes.

- **Antiseptic wipes.** They come in little packets and are used to clean wounds before bandaging. Some contain alcohol and sting; others are pain-free.

- **Antibiotic ointment.** This is essential to put on any wound or cut to keep it from becoming infected. It doesn't sting and can be purchased in a tube or tiny packets.

- **Adhesive bandages.** Commonly called Band-Aids, these are important for keeping small wounds covered and clean. Get a variety of sizes and shapes.

- **Butterfly bandages.** These are small, strong adhesive bandages in a butterfly shape that will hold deeper cuts closed and stop bleeding. Pinch the cut closed and tape them tightly across the wound.

- **Small rolled elastic bandage.** Also known as an Ace bandage, this is used to wrap injured joints such as ankles and wrists.

- **Medical adhesive tape.** It comes in many forms. Get a type that can be torn by hand instead of cut so you do not have to carry scissors.

- **Hand sanitizer.**

- **Hydrocortisone cream.** Use it to treat the itchiness, redness, swelling, and pain of bug bites and stings, poison ivy, or similar skin reactions.

- **Antihistamine and EpiPen.** Many people carry the antihistamine Benadryl (diphenhydramine), which stops allergic reactions, such as those caused by bee stings or fire ant bites. Benadryl makes most people sleepy, but it can be a lifesaver. It is even good for dogs that have been stung by bees; a very small dog needs only a quarter tablet, a medium-size dog a half a tablet, and a large dog one tablet. Talk to your parents about putting a few tablets in your first-aid kit. In addition, if you or someone close to you is badly allergic to bee stings, talk to your doctor about carrying an EpiPen, which is an emergency treatment for severe allergic reactions.

- **Antidiarrhea pills and stomach-soothing pills**.

- **Pain-relief tablets**. A few pain-relief tablets can be very valuable in the event of an injury, like a broken bone or burn. However, kids and teens who have a possible viral illness should not take aspirin; it can cause Reye's syndrome, which is a rare but serious disease. Better choices for your first-aid kit are other painkillers: ibuprofen (Advil, Motrin, and others), naproxen (Aleve), or acetaminophen (Tylenol and others). Talk to your parents about choosing the pain-relief medication that is best for you.

- **Sling**. You can buy a sling with safety pins to attach it to prepare for the possibility of an arm injury. It can also be used as an ankle brace if you tie it tightly around your foot and ankle.

- **Tweezers**. Splinters are a common problem, and they're often difficult to remove without tweezers. Tweezers are also handy for tick removal.

- **Needle.** For removing splinters underneath the skin.
- **Poison oak, ivy, and sumac wash.** Search and rescue workers and wild-land firefighters carry Tecnu packets when working around these irritating plants. It removes the oils that cause rashes and blisters before your skin can react to it. Rub it over your skin and wash it off with cold water.
- **Aloe vera lotion.** This plant-based lotion soothes sunburned skin.

CAR EMERGENCY KIT

Every family's car should contain an emergency kit in case they become stranded or face a natural disaster or other dangerous situation. It may never happen, but you should always be ready for an emergency. Emergency food bars that will keep you alive for weeks and last for years are great to have in your kit. A few blankets, some flares, and extra water should always be there as well, even if you live in the city. There are kits you can buy, or you can make your own.

ACTIVITY A great family project is deciding what should be in your family's emergency kit and putting it together. You may already have some items in your house or garage; others you can buy. Your kit should be tailored to the size of your family, your geographic area (mountains, desert, or city), the season, and your local hazards. For instance, if you live in Minnesota and are traveling in the winter, your kit will be much different from that of someone driving across Arizona in the summer.

In addition, it's a good idea to talk with your parents about possible emergencies in your area. Make a plan for the whole family to meet at an assigned location.

Your emergency kit could include:

- Your cell phone and charger
- Blanket
- Warm clothing (having a dry change of clothing can be a lifesaver in winter weather)
- 2 gallons of bottled water
- Flares (for road safety, but also for starting a fire for signaling and warmth)
- Flashlight and extra batteries
- Spare tire and tools (check to make sure that the spare tire isn't flat before you leave)
- Nonperishable food such as emergency food bars
- Toilet paper
- First-aid kit (see the previous section)
- Tarp
- Small shovel (for digging out of snow or mud, or digging under your car in summer to provide shade in a treeless area)

- Duct tape

Depending on the season and where you live, it may also include:

- Mosquito netting (taped over your car's windows, it can save you from the torment of mosquitoes if you are stranded in hot weather)

- Shade cloth (loosely woven Mylar fabric used by gardeners to shade plants and found at nursery supply companies; if you're stranded in a hot-weather area without shade, it's a wonderful way to reflect most of the sun and heat off your car by draping it over the roof)

- Sleeping bags (recommended for winter travel, as blankets may not be enough in snow country or extreme cold)

- Small bag of landscape gravel or kitty litter (to help you get your car out of snow or mud; you can also use your car's floor mats for traction under your tires)

RESOURCES

WEBSITES
Survival Skills

Survivor Kid
www.survivor-kid.com
This is the official *Survivor Kid* website. You can take
an animal tracks quiz, listen to wild animal sounds, find
recommendations on survival gear to buy, and test your
survival gear knowledge.

Wilderness Survival Website
www.surviveoutdoors.com
This site has an enormous menu of outdoorsy topics with
great information and pictures.

www.wilderness-survival.net/chp8.php
The Wilderness Survival website features a quiz and many
pages of useful information on survival kits, medicine,
plants, animals, and other topics.

www.equipped.org/fm21-76.htm
Instead of paying for the actual US Army Survival Guide, you can download it here for free.

Animated Knots by Grog
www.animatedknots.com/indexrescue.php
This site provides an animated guide to tying numerous types of knots and explains the uses of each one.

Navigation and Orienteering Websites

www.learn-orienteering.org
www.compassdude.com
www.geocaching.com
www.gpsnuts.com
All these sites provide information on navigation, using a compass, geocaching, and related topics, with easy-to-follow instructions and diagrams.

Magazine Websites

www.backpacker.com
www.outsideonline.com
Consider subscribing to a magazine that specializes in outdoor skills, gear, and survival, such as *Backpacker* or *Outside*. These magazines feature useful articles, equipment ratings and reviews, and helpful advice on a wide variety of topics.

Plants and Animals

USDA PLANTS Database
http://plants.usda.gov/adv_search.html
Does poison sumac grow near you? How about
blueberries? On this site, you can look up all the plants
that grow wild in the United States.

eNature
www.enature.com
This site is a great field guide. You can look up all the
plants, animals, and insects that live in your zip code,
or you can just identify poisonous plants and animals in
your area.

Nat Geo Wild: Animals
http://animals.nationalgeographic.com/animals
Learn about animals from National Geographic.

Tracking Websites

www.bear-tracker.com
www.naturetracking.com
Beartracker's Animal Tracks Den and NatureTracking are
helpful sites for learning about animal prints and scat.

Soundboard.com
www.soundboard.com
Type in the name of an animal in the search box to
download animal sounds from around the world.

Specific Locations and Animals

Alaska Department of Fish & Game:
Wildlife Conservation
http://wildlife.alaska.gov
This site provides information on moose and other
animals found in Alaska.

Arizona Game and Fish Department:
Living with Wildlife
www.azgfd.gov/w_c/urban_az_wildlife.shtml
Great guides to desert animals such as javelinas, bobcats,
mountain lions, bats, and bears.

Bear Websites

www.glacier-national-park-travel-guide.com
At the unofficial Glacier National Park Travel Guide,
learn about grizzly bears, their food, and how to be safe in
bear country.

www.nps.gov/archive/glac/resources/bears2.htm
The National Park Service's official Glacier National Park
website also has information on grizzly bears and bear
spray and has a chart comparing black and grizzly bears.

www.jasperwildlife.com
Do you want to know what a marmot is? This informative
site tells you about bears and other wildlife found in
Canada and the United States. There are also pages of
great wildlife photos.

www.cougarinfo.org
This site keeps track of mountain lion attacks and offers other great information about the big cats.

Reptile Websites

www.pitt.edu/~mcs2/herp/SoNA.html
If you are looking for photos of North American snakes, along with both their common and their scientific names, Snakes of North America is the site to visit.

www.naherpetology.org
The Center for North American Herpetology has a giant page of links to reptile and amphibian websites.

www.myfwc.com
The official website of the Florida Fish and Wildlife Conservation Commission has great information about snakes and alligators.

Spider and Insect Websites

www.bugguide.net
Everything you might want to know about spiders and insects. Tons of photos and information are available on every type of bug.

www.whatsthatbug.com
Did you find a bug you cannot identify? Send this site a photo and its staff will tell you what it is.

www.termite.com/spider-identification.html
This site has an easy guide to common spiders, especially
venomous ones.

www.insectidentification.org
On this site, you'll find large photos of common insects
and spiders with information on each one.

Wolf Websites

www.wolfechovalley.com/wolfcountry.html
This site has advice for those who live and explore
in wolf country.

http://icwdm.org/handbook/carnivor/Wolves.asp
If you want to learn more about where to find wolves,
what they eat, and their effects on livestock, visit this page
at the Internet Center for Wildlife Damage Management.

BOOKS

Scat and Tracks of North America
by James C. Halfpenny (Guilford, CT:
Falcon Guides, 2008)

This handy little guide can be carried in your pack. It
gives you a footprint and scat guide to animals found
in the United States, including snakes, mammals and
birds. There are also drawings of each animal with maps
showing where they live.

INDEX

ABOUT THE AUTHOR

DENISE LONG is a licensed private investigator, a certified crime analyst, and a teacher of wilderness survival classes for children. A former search and rescue volunteer, she continues to train German shepherds.